Bolton Wanderers Football Club Official Yearbook 2004-05

Editorial **Daniel Reuben, Paul Holliday and Keeley Temple**
Design **Daniel Anim-Kwapong, Ian Bull and Nick Thornton**
Photography **Action Images**
Copyright © Bolton Wanderers Football Club 2004. Copyright Sidan Press Ltd 2004.

Maps redrawn and based on Collins Town and Country series Copyright
Bartholomew Ltd 2004. Reproduced by permission of Harpercollins Publishers.

All information is current to 5th July 2004.

Club Directory

Bolton Wanderers Football Club,
Reebok Stadium, Burnden Way,
Bolton BL6 6JW

Tel **01204 673 673**
Fax **01204 673 773**
Email **reception@bwfc.co.uk**

Other Useful Contacts
Ticket and Membership Office
Tel **0871 871 2932**
Email **ticketsales@bwfc.co.uk**

Promotions Department
Tel **01204 673 663**
Email **promotions@bwfc.co.uk**

Corporate Sales Department
Tel **01204 673 761**
Email **sales@bwfc.co.uk**

Club Superstore
Tel **01204 673 650**
Email **shop@bwfc.co.uk**
Website **www.bwfcsuperstore.co.uk**

Communications Department
Tel **01204 673 675**
Email **publicity@bwfc.co.uk**

Football in the Community
Tel **01204 480 601**

Board Members
Chairman **Phil Gartside**
Vice Chairman **W.B. Warburton**
Directors **I. Currie, E. Davies O.B.E.,**
D. McBain, G. Seymour, G. Warburton
Honorary Vice Presidents **Dr. D. Dennard, D.**
Singleton, F. Smith JP
President/Honorary Director **Nat Lofthouse O.B.E.**
Vice Presidents **G.E. Ashworth, T. Edge,**
J. Lightbown, H.D. Warburton

Reebok

Contents

Message from Chairman Phil Gartside

Welcome to the start of our fourth successive campaign in the Barclays Premiership. This season presents Bolton Wanderers Football Club with a new challenge and I am very excited about the prospect of watching Bolton play in one of the most demanding leagues in the world.

Now that we are embarking on our best era for over 40 years, your support is going to be essential in ensuring that we continue our progress in the top flight.

Sam is building a strong and experienced team behind the scenes, as well as a strong team on the pitch. We know the Premiership will be extremely competitive, the journey will not be easy and your support and encouragement to the team and the players will be vital throughout every game and the entire season.

We hope that our new look Yearbook will prove an invaluable source of reference to you throughout the season.

It has been produced to give you an at a glance guide to a wealth of statistical knowledge about our club.

Once again, thank you for your continued support and let's enjoy the forthcoming season together.

Phil Gartside
Chairman

Message from Manager Sam Allardyce

Welcome to what I hope will be yet another fantastic season for Bolton Wanderers Football Club.

Our hard work, on the pitch and behind the scenes, was fully rewarded last term which helped us record our best finish for 44 years. We are under no illusions of how difficult it will be to emulate that feat again this coming season.

We now have a fine blend of experience and youthful talent which can only serve us well. Hopefully, we will have added a few more new faces to the squad by the time this Yearbook is published.

This season, we have published this new look Yearbook for you, our supporters. It contains everything you need to know about Bolton Wanderers Football Club and has comprehensive statistics on our players. I hope you find it informative and useful.

Finally, I'd like to thank you for your great support last season and I look forward to seeing you cheer the lads on this season.

Big Sam
Manager

Junior Whites

Bolton Wanderers Football Club relaunched its hugely successful Junior Whites Club at the beginning of the 2003/04 season..

Unlike the previous junior programme, the new Junior Whites Members Club is FREE to all youngsters under the age of 16.

This Club initiative, involves a six-figure annual investment aiming to capture the imagination and support of youngsters throughout the region.

The aim of Junior Whites is to be completely inclusive, to encourage children from all backgrounds to become active members and to enable them to experience top flight football at the Reebok Stadium.

Wanderers are amongst the first in the Premier League to offer FREE membership to junior supporters.

Thanks to the Junior Whites sponsors, Coca-Cola, Reebok and Bolton Evening News the Club will offer an exciting package of benefits.

One of the biggest benefits, which is unique to the Wanderers, is that all members on their 7th birthday will receive an official BWFC Junior replica shirt for the special price of only £10, courtesy of Associate Sponsor Reebok, giving a fantastic saving of £19.99 on the usual price.

In addition to this great benefit, members will receive the following benefits

- The opportunity to become the official team mascot at a Premier League match.
- Exclusive Junior Whites TeamCard enabling members to participate in the revolutionary BWFC loyalty scheme allowing members to collect TeamCard points at over 40 partners nationwide.
- Membership Certificate.
- Exclusive free gift.
- Voucher for a FREE tour of the Reebok Stadium
- Birthday card
- Christmas card
- Two free match tickets every season to watch the Wanderers in the Premier League
- Six newsletters per year
- Meet the players' events throughout the year
- Special away trips to events and matches around the UK
- Exclusive access to weekly football training sessions

In conjunction with Associate Sponsor and Media Partner, Kidzone @ Bolton Evening News, the Junior Whites Club will have its own exclusive column published every Friday in the BEN, giving members the chance to enter exclusive competitions.

For further information on the Junior Whites Membership Programme, please contact: **01204 673770**

Study@BWFC
What is Study@BWFC?

Study@BWFC is an out-of-hours study centre, which young people from schools all over Bolton attend on a voluntary basis. The centre aims to provide a programme of activities that complement the work of schools in raising achievement in Literacy, Numeracy and ICT, but aims to be distinctly different.

The centre has three main aims;
- To encourage pupils to believe in themselves and their own ability to achieve.
- To provide opportunities for students to become self-motivated learners and to enable them to discover new talents, skills and interests.
- To help pupils to develop the skills to learn more effectively and to think more creatively.

What is Playing for Success?

BWFC were one of the first football clubs to provide a Study Centre for their local community.

The current Study Centre was opened in March 1999 as part of the initiative, 'Playing for Success'.

The Government, in partnership with Premiership and First Division football clubs, Local Education Authorities and businesses has been establishing out of hours learning centres at football clubs all over the country.

Due to the success of the initiative, the programme has been 'rolled out' to include other sports such as cricket and rugby.

Who can attend Study@BWFC?

Students between the ages of 10 and 14 attend the centre. Schools are selected through the LEA each year and they can then select students who they feel will benefit and commit themselves to attending the centre.

Attendance at Study@BWFC is a reward for students who are already doing well in school but are prepared to put in 'extra time' to improve their levels of achievement further.

Since 1999 the Centre has helped to raise standards in Literacy, Numeracy and ICT for over 4,000 pupils in Bolton!

Which amounts to over 40,000 hours of extra work that children and young people have taken part in VOLUNTARILY!

Added to this every school in Bolton has had the opportunity to send pupils to Study@BWFC.

What happens at Study@BWFC?

The learning programme and facilities offered are distinctively different to 'school'; amongst the benefits to students are the opportunities to learn from BWFC players and to use the Reebok Stadium itself to improve their skills in many subject areas.

Sessions are fun, relaxed and informal and have proven to build self-confidence and self-esteem.

National evaluations have shown that football-based Study Centres have helped to raise mental arithmetic scores by 21 months and reading scores by 15 months!

It is clear that something remarkable happens to learners at Study@BWFC, which defies measurement or explanation.

Contact Information: **Study@BWFC, The Reebok Stadium, Burnden Way Bolton, BL6 6JW**
Tel: **01204 669911** E-mail: **info@studybwfc.co.uk** Website: **www.bwfcstudy.co.uk**

Football in the Community

Bolton Wanderers was one of the first clubs in the country to pioneer the Football In The Community scheme.

Almost 15 years later, we are still very proud to boast one of the best schemes of its kind anywhere in the county, which is down in no small measure to our Community Officer Geoff Lomax, the former Manchester City midfielder, who has been in charge since 1989.

The Community Programme, as it is officially known, was established in 1986 as a pilot scheme involving six clubs in the North West of England. Bolton was one of them. With support from The Professional Footballers' Association, The Football League, The FA Premier League and The Football Association, the scheme now supports every league club in England and Wales.

The aims of Football in the Community are to encourage more people to watch and play the game, to support their local club and improve the image of the game. We do this by concentrating on the youth of our area. These are the activities we offer: In-term Coaching, After Schools and Sponsored Events

Our in-term coaching programme is still going as strong as ever with schools such as Ladybridge, Kearsley West, Tonge Moor and Eccleston (Chorley) all having received three coaching sessions covering lots of different techniques and skills and small-sided games.

As well as the in-term coaching, our popular after-school programmes are proving to be a real success story. These involve a week long soccer course at primary schools and secondary schools where all participants receive coaching from P.F.A qualified staff.

Coaches deliver wide ranging sessions covering running with the ball to dribbling, passing, shooting and aerial control.

Depending on the time of year, the after school sessions participants receive either a complimentary match ticket to a first team BWFC fixture or a Trophy to show for their efforts!

2002 sees BWFC Football In The Community break their record for fundraising events in schools. Already we have raised valuable funds for schools such as St Matthews, St Mary's and Adlington St Pauls.

Schools have the option of participating in a sponsored 'Skills Day' (where each child learns 5 new exciting soccer skills) or a 'Penalty Shoot Out' where children take 5 penalties against members of the FITC coaching staff!

These events are hugely popular with schools who recognise how valuable they are in terms of raising much needed funds for PE equipment and other much needed resources.

Easter Soccer Courses

Over 700 boys and girls attended the 'Easter Extravaganza' soccer schools earlier this year. The varied coaching programme involved specific courses for strikers and goalkeepers as well as our ever popular 'Just Football' competitions where each player receives points regardless of whether their teams have won, drawn or lost!

On many of these courses, we were lucky enough to welcome numerous BWFC first team players who came along and joined in with the sessions!

Also included in our Easter coaching programme were courses organised by our Ethnic Minorities Community Officer Azam Makki.

Over 100 children participated at various venues across the area.

Disability Coaching:

Thanks to the FA Premier League and sponsor Barclaycard, All the staff at BWFC Football In The Community have successfully completed the F.A. 'Coaching Disabled Footballers' and our disability/special needs coaching programme is now very much under way.

Already we have visited schools such as Rumworth, Birtenshaw, Ladywood and Firwood where we delivered 'taster' sessions covering different football techniques and skills.

In addition to the in-term coaching FITC also operate a weekly 'One 2 One Ability Counts' session held each Wednesday evening at Smithills Sports Centre.

We welcome adults and children regardless of ability or playing experience, each session costs just £1.50.

So far we have coached over 60 participants in these sessions where we concentrate on including everyone and having fun whilst learning fundamentals of football at the same time!

If your school or organisation is interested in any of the disability/special needs coaching we provide please contact the community office on (01204) 698800.

Promotions

LIFELIN£

Now 21 years on, Lifeline goes from strength to strength. For just £2 a week you could be part of Lifeline. There's a chance of winning up to £2500 every week, 52 weeks per year plus the added bonus of winning the biggest cash prize ever seen in Bolton, £21,000 drawn in December 2004. Application forms are available from the Promotions Department, Club Superstore and the Ticket Office.

As a Lifeline member you also have a number of benefits which include 5% off the price of a season ticket, priority on match tickets, plus exclusive party nights. Call now on 01204 673774.

GOLDLIN£

Just £1 will guarantee your membership of the Goldline Daily Draw. £500 can be won each weekday Monday to Friday and we also give away £100's in consolation prizes every week. Can you afford not to be a member?

As a Goldline member you will also receive free entry into the National Lottery Draw for both Saturday and Wednesday, as part of a syndicate of no more than 100 members. There are various methods of payment from door to door collections to standing order direct from your bank, the choice is yours. For full details contact 01204 673772.

LOTT£RY

Now in its 24th year, our instant win scratchcards are proving to be very popular with our supporters. Each ticket offers big money prizes along with numerous exciting prizes in Sam's Treasure Chest. It all adds up to a £50,000 prize fund so make sure you are one of our many winners and buy our instant win scratchtickets.

Tickets are available in retail outlets throughout Bolton and surrounding areas. For further information contact us on 01204 673663.

GOLD£N GAMBL£

Our Golden Gamble Matchday 50/50 draw is as popular as ever. For just £1 you have the chance of walking away from the game with a cheque up to £2,000 (dependant on sales). Sellers are located at all turnstiles around the Reebok – make sure you don't miss out on your chance of winning. Visit www.bwfc.co.uk to see the results.

Walkway of Fame & Book of Remembrance

Supporters of Bolton Wanderers can become part of the history of our great club. Wanderers are offering fans the opportunity to purchase their own place of history along the Wanderers Walkway of Fame.

From just £39.99 a single brick can be inscribed with two rows of up to 16 characters. Alternatively a double brick, inscribed with up to 4 rows of 16 characters, can be purchased from £74.99. For £99 a black memorial brick can be inscribed in gold for a loved one or alternatively for £25 you can have your message entered into our Book of Remembrance which will be situated outside the Promotions Department from mid July 2004. For more details contact 01204 673663.

Travel Club

For just £5 you can join the Official BWFC Travel Club and save £££'s. Save at least £3 per booking, travel in comfort and forget about parking.

And with a new exciting Members Draw introduced this season for an exclusive "money can't buy" prize, what more reason to join?

Telephone 01204 673663 for further details.

Corporate Hospitality

The Bolton Wanderers Corporate Sales Department organises the matchday hospitality of up to 2,500 guests. From 8 or 10 seat boxes to the 700-strong Premier Suite there is a variety of availability for all requirements. The range of hospitality packages available includes the ever popular Platinum Suite and, new for 2004, the luxiourious surroundings of the Chairman's Suite to name but two.

The department also co-ordinates all in-stadia advertising including perimeter boards, matchday programme and videoscreen advertising.

In addition, the department also organises large-scale events such as the Player of the Year Dinner, Chairman's Ball and Wanderers for the Day.

Player of the Year Dinner 2005

Following the huge success of last year's event, preparations are now beginning in earnest for the fourth annual dinner. This season's event will be bigger and better with attendance by the full first team squad, directors and management of the Club.

Tickets for this event will go on sale in January 2005.

Wanderers For The Day 2005

Have you ever dreamed of playing for a Premiership side? Have you ever wanted to score the winning goal at the Reebok Stadium? Well, now's your chance!

In May 2005, Bolton Wanderers are hiring out the Reebok Stadium pitch for full 11-a-side games for teams wishing to play on the Reebok turf and follow in the footsteps of Jay Jay Okocha and Kevin Davies.

All requests should be directed through the sales team on 01204 673761 or email sales@bwfc.co.uk

Now in store -
Reebok training wear
new season's ranges

BWFC SUPERSTORE

Mailorder Hotline 0845 1249828

www.bwfc.co.uk

Mon-Weds, Fri 9am to 5pm   Thursday 9.30am to 8pm
Saturday 9am to 5pm   Sunday 11am to 5pm

EVERY penny you spend with Bolton Wanderers Superstore goes directly to your Club

Ticket Information

How to buy a match ticket?
Tickets for matches at the Reebok Stadium are available from the following sources:

In Person
We sell tickets by personal application at the ticket office. The ticket office is open from 9.30am to 5.00pm Monday to Friday. On the weekday prior to a home game the ticket office remains open until 7.00pm.

On a Saturday (non-matchday) the ticket office is open from 9.30am to 3.000m.

On a Saturday (matchday) the ticket office is open from 9.30am until 20 minutes after the final whistle.

By Phone 0871 871 2932
For ticket related enquiries, please telephone the above number. Credit card bookings using Visa, Mastercard, Switch, Delta and Amex can be made on this number.

Please note, that a £1.00 booking fee is charged on all orders. If you are booking tickets in advance, you must bring your credit card with you when collecting your tickets.

By Fax 0871 871 8183
Please state clearly the game(s) you wish to buy tickets for, the number of tickets you want, which stand you want to sit if applicable, the ticket price and your credit card details including name, address, contact telephone number, credit card number and expiry date.

Please note, that a £1.00 booking fee is charged on all orders. If you are booking tickets in advance, you must bring your credit card with you when collecting your tickets.

By Post
Please include the same details as for fax bookings, and, if paying by cheque, please include the appropriate remittance.

Send your application to: **Ticket Office, BWFC, Reebok Stadium, Burnden Way, Bolton, BL6 6JW**

For the most up to date information on ticket availability visit the official website at **www.bwfc.co.uk** We would remind all supporters to retain the ticket stubs for all home and away games that they attend this season, in case they are used for priority ticket allocation later this season.

MATCHDAY TICKET PRICES 2004/05				
Stand	Category A+	Category A	Category B	Category C
East/West Upper				
Adult	**£38.00**	**£35.00**	**£32.00**	**£29.00**
Senior Citizen	**£27.00**	**£24.00**	**£22.00**	**£20.00**
Junior	**£21.00**	**£19.00**	**£16.00**	**£14.00**
East/West Lower				
Adult	**£35.00**	**£32.00**	**£28.00**	**£25.00**
Senior Citizen	**£25.00**	**£22.00**	**£20.00**	**£17.00**
Junior	**£16.00**	**£14.00**	**£12.00**	**£10.00**
North/South Upper				
Adult	**£30.00**	**£27.00**	**£24.00**	**£21.00**
Senior Citizen	**£23.00**	**£21.00**	**£18.00**	**£16.00**
Junior	**£16.00**	**£14.00**	**£12.00**	**£10.00**
North/South Lower				
Adult	**£30.00**	**£27.00**	**£24.00**	**£21.00**
Senior Citizen	**£23.00**	**£21.00**	**£18.00**	**£16.00**
Junior	**£16.00**	**£14.00**	**£12.00**	**£10.00**
Family				
1 Adult +1 Junior	**£42.00**	**£38.00**	**£32.00**	**£26.00**
2 Adults +2 Juniors	**£84.00**	**£76.00**	**£64.00**	**£52.00**

Season Review

Manchester United 4

Premiership
Saturday 16th August 2003
Venue: **Old Trafford**
Attendance: **67,647**
Referee: **P.A.Durkin**

PREMIERSHIP FIXTURE HISTORY

Played:**5** Draws:**1**	Wins	⚽	◻	◼
Manchester United	2	9	5	0
Bolton Wanderers	2	4	10	0

STARTING LINE-UPS

Howard

P.Neville   Ferdinand   Silvestre   Fortune

Solskjaer   Keane (c)   Butt   Scholes

van Nistelrooy   Giggs

Davies

Pedersen   Stelios

Okocha (c)   Nolan

Campo

Gardner   N'Gotty   Laville   Hunt

Jaaskelainen

Ronaldo, Forlan,
Djemba-Djemba,
O'Shea, Carroll.

Djorkaeff, Facey,
Frandsen, Barness,
Poole.

PREMIERSHIP MILESTONES

Bolton had three players making their debuts; Stelios Giannakopoulos, Nicky Hunt and Kevin Davies.

It was a tough start for Wanderers, as defending champions United registered a flattering 4-0 win at Old Trafford.

For an hour the visitors matched their illustrious counterparts in every aspect, but the introduction of new signing Cristiano Ronaldo on 60 minutes proved to be decisive, as the hosts rattled in three more goals to add to Ryan Giggs's 35th-minute opener.

Jay-Jay Okocha, freshly installed as the new Wanderers captain following Gudni Bergsson's retirement, was in a determined mood and seemed to be at the heart of all the threatening moves from Sam Allardyce's men.

The Nigerian fired a thunderbolt at the United goal in the seventh minute, but it flew harmlessly wide.

On 10 minutes he found debutant Stelios with a great right-footed pass. The Greek knocked it to Kevin Nolan, who tested Tim Howard with a deft chip.

Six minutes later, Jussi Jaaskelainen showed his worth for Wanderers with a brave save at the feet of Giggs.

But Jaaskelainen couldn't do anything about Giggs's opener. The shot was sweetly struck and rebounded off the Finn's left-hand post to settle over the line.

For the early part of the second half, the game continued as it had ended in the first, with neither side causing too many problems. However, the introduction of Ronaldo on the hour mark changed the pattern of the game.

Ten minutes after his arrival, his trickery earned United a penalty when Nolan upended him in the box.

Ruud van Nistelrooy, who last season could do no wrong from the penalty spot, followed up his miss from the spot in the previous week's Community Shield victory against Arsenal with another. Credit should be given to Jaaskelainen, however, as he made an athletic dive to thwart the Dutchman's powerful drive.

That should have boosted Wanderers' confidence for the rest of the game, but a lack of concentration during a Ronaldo cross resulted in Giggs adding his and United's second.

The Portuguese whizkid's cross was knocked into the six-yard box by Paul Scholes, and while Jaaskelainen did well to parry Van Nistelrooy's point-black shot, Giggs was there to guide the ball into an empty net.

Scholes then got in on the scoring act, slotting home a controversial goal from an apparently offside position.

Van Nistelrooy, who had had a disappointing game by his usual standards, then added a flattering fourth.

0 Bolton Wanderers

Kevin Davies goes up for a header with Rio Ferdinand.

Jay-Jay Okocha fires in a free-kick.

"Everyone was disappointed with the result, but United are the Premiership champions and they showed it." – Kevin Nolan

Bolton Wanderers 2

FIXTURE INFORMATION

Premiership
Saturday 23rd August 2003
Venue: **Reebok Stadium**
Attendance: **27,423**
Referee: **A.P.D'Urso**

PREMIERSHIP FIXTURE HISTORY

	Played:5 Draws:3	Wins	⚽	☐	■
Bolton Wanderers		2	8	8	0
Blackburn Rovers		0	6	11	3

STARTING LINE-UPS

Jaaskelainen

Hunt   Laville   N'Gotty   Gardner

Nolan   Campo   Okocha (c)

Djorkaeff   Pedersen

Davies

Jansen   Yorke

Thompson   Tugay   Flitcroft (c)   Emerton

Gresko   Amoruso   Taylor   Neill

Friedel

Frandsen, Barness,   Cole, Reid,
Stelios, Jardel,   Grabbi, Johansson,
Poole.   Kelly.

PREMIERSHIP MILESTONES

Kevin Davies marked his appearance against his former club with his first goal for Bolton.

Dwight Yorke's late, late equaliser denied Wanderers their first victory of the season in this Reebok Stadium clash.

The former Manchester United hitman earned his side a point in the final minute of injury time – just as Craig Short had last season – after Matt Jansen had clawed the visitors back into the game following first-half Bolton goals from Youri Djorkaeff and Kevin Davies.

Wanderers dominated the early stages, as they worked to put the disappointment at Old Trafford behind them.

Moments after the kick-off, Djorkaeff firmly illustrated his intentions for the game with a deft chip towards the goal, but the ball flew just over Brad Friedel's bar.

The American keeper wasn't as fortunate a minute later when he faced the Frenchman from the spot, a penalty having been awarded for Lucas Neill's tug on Jay-Jay Okocha during the Nigerian World Cup star's powerful run into the box. Friedel guessed the right way, but Djorkaeff slotted home with great precision to give the hosts a morale-boosting lead.

The goal pushed Rovers onto the back foot, and Djorkaeff and Henrik Pedersen both went close to increasing the lead.

Wanderers grabbed their second on 25 minutes through Rovers old boy Davies, as the 26-year-old latched onto Okocha's superb through-ball and confidently fired past Friedel for his first goal of the season.

Pedersen could have added a third just five minutes later, but Friedel made a splendid dive to thwart the Dane.

Although they didn't make any changes in personnel, Rovers came out for the second half with a different look to them. Jansen tested Jussi Jaaskelainen just three minutes in with a well-struck volley, but the Finn comfortably gathered the ball.

But the former Carlisle United and Crystal Palace striker managed to pull a goal back four minutes later, when he converted David Thompson's smart cross.

Rovers began to increase the intensity of their attacks as they searched for a second.

Wanderers had several chances to increase the lead, but they seemed to lack a killer instinct.

Bolton received a boost in the 88th minute when Steven Reid was shown a red card for a wild tackle on Stelios.

Despite losing a man, Rovers kept launching the ball into the Wanderers box, and they were rewarded in the final minute of injury times, as Yorke collected a Ciccio Grabbi cross and powered the ball past Jaaskelainen.

"We knew Blackburn were going to throw men forward, and we just couldn't defend."
– Sam Allardyce

2 Blackburn Rovers

Youri Djorkaeff scores from the spot.

STATISTICS

This Season	This Match		This Season	This Match
12	8	Shots On Target	6	18
15	5	Shots Off Target	7	19
1	0	Hit Woodwork	0	0
5	4	Caught Offside	2	5
13	9	Corners	2	8
23	12	Fouls	18	30
42%	42%	Possession	58%	55%

PREMIERSHIP STANDINGS

Position (pos before)	W	D	L	F	A	Pts
16 (20) Bolton	0	1	1	2	6	1
3 (1) Blackburn	1	1	0	7	3	4

Ricardo Gardner moves in from the wing.

Portsmouth 4

FIXTURE INFORMATION

Premiership
Tuesday 26th August 2003
Venue: **Fratton Park**
Attendance: **20,113**
Referee: **D.J.Gallagher**

PREMIERSHIP FIXTURE HISTORY

Played:1 Draws:0	Wins	⚽	◻	◼
Portsmouth	1	4	2	0
Bolton Wanderers	0	0	4	0

STARTING LINE-UPS

Hislop

Schemmel   De Zeeuw   Stefanovic   Zivkovic

Stone   Faye   Quashie   Berger

Sheringham (c)   Yakubu

Pedersen   Davies   Djorkaeff

Okocha (c)   Campo   Frandsen

Gardner   N'Gotty   Laville   Barness

Jaaskelainen

🎽 Primus, Pericard,
Harper, O'Neil,
Wapenaar.

🎽 Charlton, Jardel,
Stelios, Nolan,
Poole.

PREMIERSHIP MILESTONES

Bolton keeper Jussi Jaaskelainen made his 75th appearance in the Premiership.

Mario Jardel started his Premiership career.

Teddy Sheringham's hat-trick sent Bolton to a crushing defeat against Premiership new boys Portsmouth.

The former Spurs hitman's three second-half goals followed Steve Stone's opener to complete a miserable night for the lacklustre Trotters.

There were few goalscoring opportunities in the first half, but Henrik Pedersen might have given Wanderers an early lead on two occasions.

Just over a minute had elapsed when compatriot Per Frandsen fired in a cross from the right. Pedersen managed to get his head to the ball, but his effort lacked direction and the ball scuttled away for a goal kick.

The Danish striker fluffed a great chance three minutes later, when he fired wide with only keeper Shaka Hislop to beat.

The hosts registered their first effort through former Liverpool star Patrik Berger. The Czech midfielder capitalised on a loose ball, but could only fire straight at Jussi Jaaskelainen.

Pompey striker Yakubu Aiyegbeni was a constant threat, and Florent Laville was booked for a foul on the pacey Nigerian.

Teddy Sheringham had a free kick within striking distance on 26 minutes, but his effort failed to trouble Jaaskelainen.

Wanderers had to wait less than a minute after the restart for their next chance to test Hislop, as Kevin Davies received the ball outside Pompey's box and hit a powerful dipping volley which required all of the Trinidad and Tobago keeper's 6ft 5in to tip away for a corner.

Portsmouth responded almost immediately, as Stone put the hosts in front after Jaaskelainen failed to clear Berger's shot.

Wanderers came close to levelling soon after, as Bruno N'Gotty flicked on Youri Djorkaeff's corner and Laville managed to get a boot to the ball, only to see it fly over the bar.

Poor play by the Wanderers defence allowed Portsmouth to double their lead on 57 minutes, as Boris Zivkovic crossed for the unmarked Sheringham, who planted a strong header past Jaaskelainen.

Wanderers boss Sam Allardyce made an attacking double substitution just past the hour mark, inserting Stelios and debutant Mario Jardel for Frandsen and Davies. The change almost had an instant impact, as Stelios knocked the ball over his head to Pedersen, whose acrobatic effort went narrowly wide.

Things went from bad to worse when Sheringham took advantage of a defensive lapse to add his second goal on 88 minutes. And he compounded Bolton's misery when he fired home from the spot two minutes later.

0 Bolton Wanderers

Anthony Barness tackles Teddy Sheringham.

EVENT LINE

13 ☐ Laville (Foul)

39 ☐ Davies (Foul)

41 ⇄ Barness (Off) Charlton (On)

HALF TIME 0-0

48 ⊙ Stone (Open Play)

57 ⊙ Sheringham (Open Play)

63 ⇄ Frandsen (Off) Jardel (On)

64 ⇄ Davies (Off) Stelios (On)

73 ☐ Zivkovic (Foul)

76 ☐ Charlton (Foul)

80 ☐ Stelios (Foul)

81 ⇄ Schemmel (Off) Primus (On)

84 ☐ Quashie (Foul)

84 ⇄ Yakubu (Off) Pericard (On)

88 ⊙ Sheringham (Open Play)

90 ⊙ Sheringham (Penalty)

FULL TIME 4-0

Kevin Davies cuts past Patrik Berger.

STATISTICS

This Season	This Match		This Season	This Match
15	9	Shots On Target	4	16
7	5	Shots Off Target	9	24
0	0	Hit Woodwork	0	1
13	8	Caught Offside	5	10
13	0	Corners	4	17
54	12	Fouls	14	37
49%	55%	Possession	45%	43%

PREMIERSHIP STANDINGS

Position (pos before)	W	D	L	F	A	Pts
1 (6) Portsmouth	2	1	0	7	2	7
19 (18) Bolton	0	1	2	2	10	1

"It was very embarrassing for our supporters, who came down on a Tuesday night to watch what was a diabolical performance." — Sam Allardyce

Bolton Wanderers 0

FIXTURE INFORMATION

Premiership
Saturday 30th August 2003
Venue: **Reebok Stadium**
Attendance: **23,098**
Referee: **A.G.Wiley**

PREMIERSHIP FIXTURE HISTORY

Played: **3** Draws: **2**	Wins	⚽	⬜	⬛
Bolton Wanderers	0	1	6	0
Charlton Athletic	1	2	5	0

STARTING LINE-UPS

Jaaskelainen

Hunt   Laville   Thome   Gardner

Nolan   Campo   Okocha (c)

Djorkaeff   Pedersen

Davies

Bartlett   Euell

Jensen   Parker   Holland (c)   Kishishev

Hreidarsson   Fortune   Fish   Young

Kiely

Stelios, Charlton, Frandsen, Facey, Poole.

Johansson, Lisbie, Powell, Stuart, Royce.

PREMIERSHIP MILESTONES

Emerson Thome made his debut in the Bolton defence after his free transfer from Sunderland.

Wanderers earned their first clean sheet of the season as they battled to a 0-0 draw against Charlton Athletic.

A combination of bad luck and good goalkeeping from Addicks keeper Dean Kiely denied the hosts a deserved three points.

Despite fielding only three changes, Wanderers looked a different outfit from the side that suffered what Sam Allardyce had called an "embarrassing and diabolical defeat" at Portsmouth in midweek.

The first half presented relatively few scoring chances for either team.

Bolton captain Jay-Jay Okocha went closest to breaking the deadlock in the seventh minute, rattling the underside of Kiely's crossbar with a free kick from 20 yards.

Charlton, always dangerous on the counter, got their first sniff of a chance on 20 minutes, as the impressive midfielder Scott Parker raced clear on goal, only to be dispossessed by local youngster Nicky Hunt before he could muster a shot.

Wanderers suffered another scare just eight minutes later, when Shaun Bartlett headed the ball over from Claus Jensen's free kick.

A chance fell Ricardo Gardner's way in the 39th minute, as Youri Djorkaeff ghosted in behind the Addicks defence to sneak in a cross. The ball was only partially cleared before finding its way to the Jamaican, whose shot through a crowd was gathered by Kiely.

Jussi Jaaskelainen had to be at his most alert moments later, saving splendidly after Matt Holland had beaten the offside trap.

Inserting Stelios for Henrik Pedersen during the interval proved to be an inspired substitution by Sam Allardyce, and Wanderers started to dominate the game in the second half.

Stelios got a long-range shot on target just before the hour mark, but his effort lacked power and was safely gathered by Kiely.

Kevin Davies, who was his usual industrious self throughout, was proving a great target man for Wanderers' direct balls.

Kiely made another great save to thwart Stelios on 69 minutes, before Wanderers had two penalty claims waved away in quick succession, both incidents involving Davies and Addicks defender Luke Young.

Djorkaeff forced Kiely into another fine save in the 74th minute, before Okocha fired a shot just inches wide.

Djorkaeff was determined to grab what would have been his fifth goal in four games against the Londoners, and he was so nearly rewarded in the 78th minute when a goalbound effort was cleared off the line by Hermann Hreidarsson.

0 Charlton Athletic

Henrik Pedersen passes under pressure from Luke Young.

"We put the opposition under great pressure, but our finishing wasn't clinical enough to get the goal we needed."
— Sam Allardyce

EVENT LINE

13 ☐ Hreidarsson (Foul)
37 ☐ Davies (Foul)
45 ☐ Jaaskelainen (Dissent)

HALF TIME 0-0

46 ⇄ Pedersen (Off) Stelios (On)
62 ☐ Fortune (Dissent)
64 ☐ Campo (Foul)
66 ⇄ Bartlett (Off) Johansson (On)
77 ⇄ Jensen (Off) Lisbie (On)
84 ☐ Okocha (Foul)

FULL TIME 0-0

STATISTICS

This Season	This Match		This Season	This Match
22	6	Shots On Target	1	18
31	7	Shots Off Target	6	20
2	1	Hit Woodwork	0	0
11	1	Caught Offside	3	13
29	12	Corners	3	15
58	21	Fouls	19	58
45%	50%	Possession	50%	49%

PREMIERSHIP STANDINGS

Position (pos before)	W	D	L	F	A	Pts
17 (19) Bolton	0	2	2	2	0	2
10 (8) Charlton	1	2	1	6	5	5

Bolton Wanderers 2

FIXTURE INFORMATION

Premiership
Saturday 13th September 2003
Venue: **Reebok Stadium**
Attendance: **26,419**
Referee: **P.Dowd**

PREMIERSHIP FIXTURE HISTORY

Played: **4** Draws: **1**	Wins	🙂	⬜	⬛
Bolton Wanderers	3	6	9	0
Middlesbrough	0	2	11	1

STARTING LINE-UPS

🥅 N'Gotty, Frandsen, Pedersen, Jardel, Poole.

👕 Ricketts, Job, Stockdale, Doriva, Nash.

An opening score from Kevin Davies put Wanderers on track for their first victory of the campaign.

The former Southampton and Blackburn Rovers striker powered home a header directly from Stelios's corner to earn Wanderers a much-deserved three points.

Substitute Bruno N'Gotty also got on the scoresheet when he netted his first of the season with 10 minutes to go.

Although Wanderers did enough during the course of the game to earn the win, Middlesbrough looked the more likely to break the deadlock during the early stages.

First, Jussi Jaaskelainen had to be alert to deny debutant Bolo Zenden's seventh-minute strike.

Jonathan Greening forced the Wanderers keeper into another save four minutes later, after Jay-Jay Okocha had flashed an effort wide just seconds earlier.

But it was Wanderers who made the breakthrough on 23 minutes, when an unmarked Davies powered his header past keeper Mark Schwarzer. Danny Mills earned a booking for protesting that the Stelios corner which led to the goal shouldn't have been awarded.

The home side suffered a blow two minutes later when Florent Laville had to be stretchered off with a knee injury. N'Gotty – fit again after recovering from a hamstring injury – came on for his compatriot.

The visitors might have equalised when a fine ball from Juninho split the Wanderers defence, opening space for Slovakian international Szilard Nemeth to power a shot towards goal. But Jaaskelainen stood tall and blocked the ball with his chest to preserve Wanderers' advantage.

Former Wanderers striker Michael Ricketts was a half-time replacement for Nemeth, but he had little joy against his old team-mates.

As the second half got underway, Wanderers were clearly the more confident and fluid side, while Middlesbrough were doing little to trouble the home defence.

If anyone was going to score it was Wanderers, and they eventually did with nine minutes to go.

Okocha's throw-in found Stelios, who hooked the ball over his head and into the box for an unchallenged N'Gotty to head past Schwarzer. N'Gotty earned a booking for running into the crowd to celebrate his third goal in Wanderers colours.

Henrik Pedersen should have added a third, but his weak right-footed effort was easily picked up by the Boro keeper.

Jaaskelainen then made a smart save to deny Ricketts' point-blank header in the final minute of time.

0 Middlesbrough

Bruno N'Gotty celebrates his goal with the fans.

Event Line

23 ⦿ Davies (Corner)

24 ☐ Mills (Dissent)

28 ⇄ Laville (Off) N'Gotty (On)

38 ☐ Gardner (Foul)

40 ☐ Cooper (Foul)

45 ☐ Djorkaeff (Foul)

HALF TIME 1-0

46 ⇄ Nemeth (Off) Ricketts (On)

50 ☐ Thome (Ung Conduct)

50 ☐ Zenden (Ung Conduct)

57 ⇄ Juninho (Off) Job (On)

69 ⇄ Hunt (Off) Frandsen (On)

75 ⇄ Djorkaeff (Off) Pedersen (On)

81 ⦿ N'Gotty (Open Play)

FULL TIME 2-0

STATISTICS

This Season	This Match		This Season	This Match
26	4	Shots On Target	6	26
37	6	Shots Off Target	1	31
2	0	Hit Woodwork	0	0
12	1	Caught Offside	6	20
39	10	Corners	1	20
78	20	Fouls	16	78
45%	47%	Possession	53%	50%

PREMIERSHIP STANDINGS

Position (pos before)	W	D	L	F	A	Pts
14 (17) Bolton	1	2	2	4	10	5
19 (19) Middlesbro	0	1	4	4	12	1

Stelios gathers the ball under pressure from Jonathan Greeening.

"We'll return to work on Monday and prepare for Newcastle, having steadied the nerves of everybody." — Sam Allardyce

Newcastle United 0

FIXTURE INFORMATION

Premiership
Saturday 20th September 2003
Venue: **St James' Park**
Attendance: **52,014**
Referee: **G.P.Barber**

PREMIERSHIP FIXTURE HISTORY

Played:**5** Draws:**1**	Wins	⚽	⬜	⬛
Newcastle United	4	8	4	0
Bolton Wanderers	0	4	6	0

STARTING LINE-UPS

Given

Griffin   Woodgate   Bramble   Bernard

Solano   Dyer   Speed   Robert

Bellamy   Shearer (c)

Davies

Djorkaeff   Stelios

Okocha (c)   Campo   Nolan

Gardner   Charlton   Thome   N'Gotty

Jaaskelainen

Jenas, Ameobi,
Hughes, Bowyer,
Caig.

Pedersen, Hunt,
Frandsen, Jardel,
Poole.

PREMIERSHIP MILESTONES

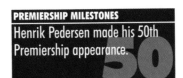

Henrik Pedersen made his 50th
Premiership appearance.

A solid defensive display from Wanderers saw them register their third consecutive clean sheet in a 0-0 draw at Newcastle.

Simon Charlton, replacing the injured Florent Laville, was outstanding in the centre of defence, keeping a firm hold on Alan Shearer throughout the game.

The hosts almost grabbed the lead after two minutes, when Emerson Thome was called for a foul on Shearer out on the right. Laurent Robert's in-swinging free kick found the head of Gary Speed, whose effort rebounded off the bar for a Wanderers goal kick.

Kevin Nolan went close for the visitors in the ninth minute, when his low drive flew narrowly wide of Shay Given's left-hand post.

Just three minutes later and Jussi Jaaskelainen had to have his wits about him to gather Andy Griffin's low, long-range drive.

The Magpies had Given to thank on 14 minutes when he made a smart save to deny Jay-Jay Okocha. The Wanderers captain's free kick from 18 yards was destined for the bottom-right corner until the Irish keeper turned it away.

Thome had to be at his most resolute in the 26th minute when Nolberto Solano's cross found Craig Bellamy, whose knock-back was heading for Shearer until the Brazilian centre-back cleared the danger.

Kevin Davies might have put the visitors ahead on the half-hour mark when Okocha's free kick found the unmarked striker in the Magpies box. But his move to control the ball on his chest gave the Toon defence time to regroup and clear the danger.

Shearer went close to scoring his 250th career goal seven minutes before the break.

He got past Thome and Bruno N'Gotty after latching onto a long ball, but the French defender regained some ground and caught the Magpies skipper with a great tackle.

The woodwork once again thwarted the hosts 12 minutes into the second period. This time Titus Bramble was left cursing his luck after seeing his header off Bellamy's hopeful hoist hit the bar.

Newcastle had a good chance five minutes from time when substitute Shola Ameobi turned past N'Gotty on the edge of the box and found Kieron Dyer in a great position with a low cross. But Charlton denied him with a strong tackle.

A draw never really seemed in doubt, however, and Wanderers deservedly claimed a share of the spoils.

"It's now three clean sheets on the trot. If we can keep in that vein, we're certainly going to start moving up and not down."
— Sam Allardyce

0 Bolton Wanderers

Ricardo Gardner gets ahead of Craig Bellamy.

Ivan Campo keeps the ball away from Gary Speed.

EVENT LINE

HALF TIME 0-0

67 ▢ Stelios (Foul)

68 ⇄ Stelios (Off) Pedersen (On)

77 ▢ Dyer (Dissent)

78 ⇄ Speed (Off) Jenas (On)

79 ⇄ Solano (Off) Ameobi (On)

87 ⇄ Djorkaeff (Off) Frandsen (On)

FULL TIME 0-0

STATISTICS

This Season	This Match		This Season	This Match
17	2	Shots On Target	5	31
29	9	Shots Off Target	3	40
2	2	Hit Woodwork	0	2
15	2	Caught Offside	5	17
38	16	Corners	5	44
84	16	Fouls	12	90
55%	59%	Possession	41%	44%

PREMIERSHIP STANDINGS

Position (pos before)	W	D	L	F	A	Pts
18 (18) Newcastle	0	3	2	5	7	3
12 (15) Bolton	1	3	2	4	10	6

Bolton Wanderers 3

Carling Cup 2nd Round
Wednesday 24th September
Venue: **Reebok Stadium**
Attendance: **5,229**
Referee: **R.Pearson**

STARTING LINE-UPS

Poole

Hunt   N'Gotty   Charlton   Barness

Nolan   Frandsen   Okocha (c)

Ba   Pedersen

Jardel

Burton

Merson (c)

Corica   Samways   Osborn   Lawrence

Aranalde   Ritchie   Emblen   Bazeley

Walker

Bon, Gardner
Stelios, Davies,
Comyn-Platt

Kerr, Taylor, Birch
Fryatt, Leitao

"When Mario gets the ball, you can see the deft flicks and all the one-touch lay-offs which will cause Premiership defences lots of problems. "
— Sam Allardyce

Mario Jardel scored twice in an inspired Wanderers debut to help Bolton progress into the next round of the Carling Cup.

The Brazilian striker, who hit 150 goals in 146 games for Porto, opened the scoring in the 15th minute with a smart header, and then fired home the rebound after his spot kick was saved by Walsall keeper James Walker.

Kevin Nolan also got on the scoresheet with a spectacular strike in the 69th minute, and Paul Merson struck what proved to be a consolation goal for the visitors five minutes later.

Despite never really being in top gear, Wanderers were still a cut above their First Division opposition.

Sam Allardyce made seven changes to the side, giving home debuts to Jardel and Ibrahim Ba.

The Saddlers' Aussie midfielder Steve Corica carved out the first chance of the game with a powerful strike, only to be denied by an athletic save from Kevin Poole, who was in for the resting Jussi Jaaskelainen.

Wanderers skipper Jay-Jay Okocha then went close with a 25-yard curler, before Jardel hit his first goal in the English game.

Fellow new boy Ba knocked Per Frandsen's cross into the path of the Brazilian, who placed his header past Walker.

Jardel was an increasingly important part of Wanderers' attacking forays, and he was unlucky not to convert Henrik Pedersen's cross three minutes from the interval, and again in the 56th minute after Pedersen's mazy run down the left.

Thirteen minutes later Pedersen lined up a shot for Nolan, whose outstanding strike sailed past Walker into the top corner. It was the midfielder's first goal of the season.

Merson gave the visitors hope as he timed his run to perfection as he converted Garry Birch's left-wing cross.

The game looked over when former Wanderer Paul Ritchie was adjudged to have handled inside his own box. Jardel's first effort was spectacularly saved by Walker, but he promptly followed up to smash the rebound home.

Jardel was unfortunate not to claim a hat-trick when his first-time left-footed volley went over the bar.

Academy youngster Charlie Comyn-Platt was given his first-team debut with nine minutes to go as Wanderers cruised into the next round.

1 Walsall

Kevin Nolan celebrates with Henrik Pedersen and Mario Jardel.

Per Frandsen takes on Vinny Samways.

EVENT LINE

KICK OFF

15 ⚽ Jardel (Open Play)

34 ▯ Barness (Foul)

HALF TIME 1-0

46 🔃 Ba (Off) Stelios (On)

46 🔃 Okocha (Off) Gardner (On)

58 🔃 Burton (Off) Birch (On)

67 🔃 Corica (Off) Fryatt (On)

69 ⚽ Nolan (Open Play)

74 ⚽ Merson (Open Play)

76 ▯ Hunt (Foul)

80 ⚽ Jardel (Penalty)

81 🔃 N'Gotty (Off) Comyn-Platt (On)

FULL TIME 3-1

STATISTICS

👕		👕
8	Shots On Target	5
9	Shots Off Target	2
1	Hit Woodwork	0
5	Caught Offside	5
9	Corners	3
8	Fouls	7

 # Bolton Wanderers 1

Premiership
Saturday 27th September 2003
Venue: Reebok Stadium
Attendance: 27,043
Referee: M.L.Dean

PREMIERSHIP FIXTURE HISTORY

Played:1 Draws:1	Wins ☉	⬜	⬛
Bolton Wanderers	0	1	2	0
Wolves	0	1	0	0

STARTING LINE-UPS

Jaaskelainen

N'Gotty   Thome   Charlton   Gardner

Nolan   Campo   Okocha (c)

Pedersen   Davies   Djorkaeff

Iversen

Kennedy   Newton

Rae   Cameron   Ince (c)

Naylor   Butler   Craddock   Irwin

Oakes

Jardel, Frandsen, Little, Hunt, Poole.

Miller, Okoronkwo, Kachloul, Murray, Gudjonsson.

PREMIERSHIP MILESTONES

Glen Little, on loan from First Division Burnley, made his Premiership debut.

Kevin Davies' third goal of the season five minutes from time preserved Wanderers' 11-game unbeaten home record after Alex Rae's first-half strike looked to have given Wolves their first ever Premiership victory.

Wanderers had two early chances to open the scoring, but Davies and Henrik Pedersen lacked the necessary precision to beat visiting keeper Michael Oakes.

Davies latched onto Ivan Campo's hopeful upfield punt and controlled the ball nicely, only to stab the ball wide. Pedersen, meanwhile, was the victim of a great block from Oakes, who raced into the path of the Dane just as he was shooting goalwards.

But it was Wolves who broke the deadlock on 30 minutes with Rae's sensational strike.

The Scottish midfielder gathered Jay-Jay Okocha's clearance from Mark Kennedy's corner and thumped the ball past Jussi Jaaskelainen for only Wolves' second goal of the season.

Buoyed by their score, the visitors began playing with a confidence which belied their position at the bottom of the table, while Wanderers looked out of sorts, their play lacking the usual fluency and accuracy of passing.

Following the restart, the visitors welcomed Scottish striker Kenny Miller – making his first appearance of the season following a hernia operation – on for the injured Steffen Iversen.

On the hour mark, Sam Allardyce brought on Brazilian Mario Jardel, who had scored twice in midweek, for Pedersen, and Per Frandsen for Campo to sharpen Wanderers' attacking play.

The substitutions almost paid off immediately, Jardel forcing Oakes into a save with an impudent toe-poke.

A few minutes later and Wanderers had Kevin Nolan to thank for preventing Wolves' second.

Jaaskelainen was forced out of the box to halt Colin Cameron's progress, but the ball fell to fellow Scot Miller, whose first-time effort was heading for goal until Nolan's acrobatic clearance off the line.

Wanderers seemed to step up a gear following the double substitution and increasingly dominated the last quarter of the match.

Okocha went very close on 70 minutes when his left-footer forced Oakes into parrying for a corner, while Emerson Thome's downwards header off Youri Djorkaeff's corner was also tipped away by Oakes.

Jardel shot wide on 81 minutes after receiving Glen Little's flick-on off Djorkaeff's corner.

And then up popped Davies in the nick of time to prevent what would have been an embarrassing defeat.

1 Wolves ⬡

Kevin Nolan gets tangled up with Steffen Iversen.

EVENT LINE

30 ⚽ Rae (Corner)

36 ☐ Nolan (Foul)

45 ☐ Thome (Foul)

HALF TIME 0-1

46 ⇄ Iversen (Off) Miller (On)

60 ⇄ Pedersen (Off) Jardel (On)

61 ⇄ Campo (Off) Frandsen (On)

79 ⇄ N'Gotty (Off) Little (On)

85 ⚽ Davies (Open Play)

86 ⇄ Newton (Off) Kachloul (On)

FULL TIME 1-1

STATISTICS

This Season	This Match		This Season	This Match
38	7	Shots On Target	4	16
52	12	Shots Off Target	4	46
2	0	Hit Woodwork	0	3
17	0	Caught Offside	5	19
56	12	Corners	3	20
105	15	Fouls	7	106
45%	51%	Possession	49%	48%

PREMIERSHIP STANDINGS

Position (pos before)	W	D	L	F	A	Pts
13 (12) Bolton	1	4	2	5	11	7
20 (20) Wolves	0	2	5	2	18	2

Kevin Davies equalises with five minutes left.

"I was disappointed that we drew the game, but pleased with the amount of pressure we put on the opposition in the second half." — Sam Allardyce

Aston Villa 1

FIXTURE INFORMATION

Premiership
Sunday 5th October 2003
Venue: **Villa Park**
Attendance: **30,229**
Referee: **R.Styles**

PREMIERSHIP FIXTURE HISTORY

Played: **5** Draws: **1**	Wins	⚽	◻	◼
Aston Villa	3	8	7	0
Bolton Wanderers	1	6	11	0

STARTING LINE-UPS

Sorensen
Delaney Mellberg (c) Alpay Samuel
McCann Barry
Hendrie Whittingham
Vassell Angel
Davies
Stelios Nolan
Okocha (c) Campo Frandsen
Gardner Charlton Thome N'Gotty
Jaaskelainen

Allback, De la Cruz,   Jardel, Little,
Kinsella, Dublin,   Hunt, Pedersen,
Postma.   Poole.

PREMIERSHIP MILESTONES

Kevin Nolan made his 75th Premiership appearance. 75

Jussi Jaaskelainen's second penalty save of the season five minutes from time earned Wanderers a point after Juan Pablo Angel had cancelled out Kevin Nolan's second-half opener.

With Per Frandsen making a rare start in place of the injured Youri Djorkaeff, Nolan was pushed up into an attacking position on the right, where he partnered Kevin Davies and fit-again Stelios.

The opening quarter-hour provided very little entertainment, but the game exploded into life on 16 minutes when Angel's edge-of-the-box free kick hit Jussi Jaaskelainen's bar. The ball rebounded into play and found its way back to the Colombian striker before Wanderers finally cleared.

Davies went close on the half-hour mark when he deflected Jay-Jay Okocha's powerful shot over the bar.

Angel had another free kick moments later, but he hit it straight at Jaaskelainen.

Okocha had a glorious chance to open the scoring 10 minutes before the interval, but his shot from the edge of the box flew over Thomas Sorensen's bar.

Stelios had a good chance seconds before the half-time whistle when the ball broke for him on the edge of the box, but he couldn't steer it past the advancing Sorensen.

Stefan Postma replaced the injured Danish keeper during the interval, and his first job was to pick the ball out of the back of the net when Nolan opened the scoring just seconds after the restart with a fantastic turn and volley for his first league goal of the season.

Ivan Campo might have doubled that lead just a minute later when he rose unmarked to meet Stelios's corner, only to miss with his header.

The hosts drew level on 58 minutes, when Angel collected the ball and played a smart one-two with Gareth Barry, before placing a curling right-footer past Jaaskelainen.

Stelios – a major problem for the Villa defence throughout – almost restored Wanderers' lead on the hour mark, but his first-time effort hit the side netting with Postma well beaten.

Wanderers had a lucky escape when Angel saw two efforts cleared off the line in the space of a couple of seconds.

Nolan, who was having an amazing second half, then carved out an opportunity for Davies with a great lay-off, but the Wanderers striker saw his effort flash wide of Postma's left-hand post.

And with five minutes to go, Jaaskelainen earned Wanderers the point with a fantastic penalty save after Campo had upended Angel in his own box.

1 Bolton Wanderers

Lee Hendrie takes on Jay-Jay Okocha

Kevin Nolan lines up a shot.

"I could feel it coming. I was well happy it did." – Kevin Nolan on his goal

EVENT LINE

HALF TIME 0-0

46 ⇄ Sorensen (Off) Postma (On)

46 ⚽ Nolan (Open Play)

55 ▯ Thome (Foul)

56 ⇄ Whittingham (Off) Allback (On)

58 ⚽ Angel (Open Play)

78 ▯ Okocha (Foul)

80 ⇄ Nolan (Off) Jardel (On)

84 ▯ Frandsen (Foul)

85 ▯ Campo (Foul)

89 ▯ Hendrie (Dissent)

90 ▯ Gardner (Foul)

90 ⇄ Stelios (Off) Little (On)

FULL TIME 1-1

STATISTICS

This Season	This Match		This Season	This Match
36	4	Shots On Target	3	41
47	10	Shots Off Target	10	62
3	2	Hit Woodwork	0	2
36	6	Caught Offside	2	19
62	10	Corners	5	61
136	13	Fouls	17	122
46%	47%	Possession	53%	46%

PREMIERSHIP STANDINGS

Position (pos before)	W	D	L	F	A	Pts
14 (15) Aston Villa	2	2	4	8	12	8
15 (17) Bolton	1	5	2	6	12	8

 # Manchester City 6

FIXTURE INFORMATION

Premiership
Saturday 18th October 2003
Venue: **City of Manchester Stadium**
Attendance: **47,101**
Referee: **S.G.Bennett**

PREMIERSHIP FIXTURE HISTORY

	Wins	⚽	⬜	⬛
Played:**3** Draws:**0**				
Manchester City	3	9	1	1
Bolton Wanderers	0	2	6	0

STARTING LINE-UPS

Seaman

Sun Jihai   Sommeil   Distin (c)   Tarnat

Reyna   Barton

Wright-Phillips   McManaman

Anelka   Fowler

Davies

Stelios   Nolan

Okocha (c)   Campo   Frandsen

Gardner   Charlton   Thome   N'Gotty

Jaaskelainen

Dunne, Sibierski,
Tiatto, Wanchope,
Stuhr-Ellegaard.

Barness, Little,
Jardel, Pedersen,
Poole.

"We didn't show the fighting spirit to see the game through – that's why we lost so heavily."

— Jay-Jay Okocha

Wanderers' recent revival on their travels came to a crashing halt as Manchester City fired six goals past them.

Wanderers returned to action after a fortnight's absence with the same starting 11 that had earned a draw against Aston Villa.

Wanderers had two good chances to take the lead in the opening two minutes.

First, Stelios forced former England keeper David Seaman into a great point-blank save. Then, a little over a minute later, Bruno N'Gotty glanced the Greek international's free kick to the wrong side of Seaman's left-hand post.

City mounted their first serious attack on 22 minutes, as Robbie Fowler's goalbound effort took a deflection for a corner.

The visitors took a deserved lead on 24 minutes. Sylvain Distin's attempted clearance finding Kevin Nolan, who guided the ball past Seaman for his second goal in as many games.

City took just two minutes to respond, however, as Shaun Wright-Phillips ghosted down the right and lobbed an advancing Jussi Jaaskelainen.

Ivan Campo wasted the best chance of the half on 37 minutes when, unmarked and with the goal at his mercy, he headed Simon Charlton's in-swinging cross inches away from Seaman's left-hand post.

Two minutes after the interval and City moved into the lead, as Nicolas Anelka ran down the left wing and crossed for Distin, who fired past Jaaskelainen.

Wright-Phillips hit his second – and City's third – on 56 minutes, Claudio Reyna playing a diagonal ball into the path of the youngster, whose first-time effort flew past Jaaskelainen.

Anelka got on the scoresheet two minutes later. Antoine Sibierski – on the field for less than 30 seconds – played his team-mate down the left, and the former Arsenal hitman's effort somehow beat Jaaskelainen on the near post for City's fourth.

Wanderers, down but not out, then pulled one back in stunning fashion, as Campo made amends for his first-half miss with an exquisite left-footer past Seaman just before the hour-mark.

Things looked even more promising for the visitors just a couple of minutes later, when Wright-Phillips, City's main attacking threat, was shown a red card for a terrible challenge on Charlton.

But despite their numerical disadvantage, City moved further ahead on 72 minutes, as Anelka latched onto a defence-splitting through-ball to slot home his side's fifth.

And Reyna completed the misery for Big Sam's men on 84 minutes when he side-footed the ball past Jaaskelainen.

2 Bolton Wanderers

Kevin Nolan and Stelios enjoy the opening goal.

Emerson Thome keeps control under pressure from Robbie Fowler.

EVENT LINE

1	▢	Davies (Foul)
24	⚽	**Nolan (Open Play)**
26	⚽	Wright-Phillips (Open Play)
27	▢	Wright-Phillips (Ung Conduct)

HALF TIME 1-1

47	⚽	Distin (Open Play)
53	🔄	**Frandsen (Off) Jardel (On)**
56	⚽	Wright-Phillips (Open Play)
56	🔄	McManaman (Off) Sibierski (On)
58	⚽	Anelka (Open Play)
59	⚽	**Campo (Open Play)**
62	▥	Wright-Phillips (Foul)
67	🔄	Fowler (Off) Tiatto (On)
72	⚽	Anelka (Open Play)
74	🔄	Barton (Off) Dunne (On)
78	🔄	**Thome (Off) Little (On)**
84	⚽	Reyna (Open Play)

FULL TIME 6-2

STATISTICS

This Season	This Match		This Season	This Match
61	13	Shots On Target	8	49
55	3	Shots Off Target	4	66
3	0	Hit Woodwork	0	2
33	2	Caught Offside	2	21
55	7	Corners	4	65
114	11	Fouls	8	130
46%	58%	Possession	42%	41%

PREMIERSHIP STANDINGS

Position (pos before)		W	D	L	F	A	Pts
4 (6)	Man City	4	3	2	20	11	15
16 (15)	Bolton	1	5	3	8	18	8

Bolton Wanderers 0

Premiership
Saturday 25th October 2003
Venue: **Reebok Stadium**
Attendance: **25,023**
Referee: **C.J.Foy**

PREMIERSHIP FIXTURE HISTORY

	Played:**2** Draws:**0**	Wins ⚽	☐	■
Bolton Wanderers	1	4	3	0
Birmingham City	1	3	4	0

STARTING LINE-UPS

Jaaskelainen

N'Gotty   Thome   Charlton   Gardner

Frandsen   Campo   Okocha (c)

Nolan   Stelios

Davies

Dugarry   Forssell

Lazaridis   Clemence   Cisse   Dunn

Clapham   Upson   Cunningham (c)   Tebily

Mai Taylor

Jardel, Pedersen, Little, Barness, Poole.

Morrison, Hughes, Kenna, Figueroa, Bennett.

Mikael Forssell ended Wanderers' unbeaten home run in a game the hosts dominated.

An unchanged line-up from the previous week seemed to have put the debacle at the City of Manchester Stadium behind them, but despite some hard graft, they couldn't find a way to the Birmingham net.

The game was generally even, but Forssell, on loan from Chelsea, made Wanderers pay for their only real mistake of the game.

Summer signing David Dunn grabbed the ball in midfield and fed Christophe Dugarry on the left. As the Frenchman weaved his way into the Bolton box, Simon Charlton slipped on the greasy surface and failed to clear the ball, allowing Forssell to slot home past compatriot Jussi Jaaskelainen after 31 minutes.

Wanderers created their first chance after three minutes, when Ricardo Gardner raced down the left to cross for Kevin Davies, only for the striker to steer his header into the arms of keeper Maik Taylor.

Gardner was also involved in Wanderers' next chance, hitting a low cross-shot into the path of Kevin Nolan, who just failed to make a connection.

In a game with numerous penalty appeals, Dunn went down under the challenge of Ivan Campo just after Forssell had put his side in front. Referee Chris Foy saw through it, however, and booked the former Blackburn man for diving.

Wanderers then had their best chance of the half, as Jay-Jay Okocha's unintended pass fell into the path of Davies, whose powerful strike was heading for goal until Taylor made a spectacular save to turn it over the top.

Okocha wasted another opportunity on 52 minutes when he fired the ball over the bar from a good position.

Stelios tried an overhead kick of Okocha's long-range throw-in seven minutes later, but the ball cleared the bar.

Birmingham were defending well as a unit and Wanderers were finding it difficult to break them down.

Sam Allardyce tried a substitution in the 65th minute, inserting Mario Jardel for Campo.

Wanderers finally found the back of the net with Stelios's stupendous bicycle kick, but his effort was correctly ruled out for offside.

Allardyce introduced Henrik Pedersen and Glen Little late in the game as his side pressed for a deserved equaliser, but Birmingham held firm to send Wanderers to their first home defeat since January.

"It was a fantastic, committed performance, especially after last week, but we just couldn't get the goal we needed."
— Simon Charlton

1 Birmingham City

Stelios tries an overhead kick.

EVENT LINE

31 ⊙ Forssell (Open Play)

34 ☐ Dunn (Ung Conduct)

44 ☐ Tebily (Foul)

HALF TIME 0-1

54 ☐ **Stelios (Ung Conduct)**

58 ⮂ Tebily (Off) Kenna (On)

65 ⮂ **Campo (Off) Jardel (On)**

77 ⮂ Lazaridis (Off) Hughes (On)

81 ⮂ **Stelios (Off) Pedersen (On)**

84 ⮂ **Nolan (Off) Little (On)**

88 ⮂ Dugarry (Off) Morrison (On)

FULL TIME 0-1

STATISTICS

This Season	This Match		This Season	This Match
51	2	Shots On Target	9	43
69	3	Shots Off Target	3	47
2	0	Hit Woodwork	0	3
27	6	Caught Offside	1	22
68	3	Corners	17	49
146	16	Fouls	5	149
42%	51%	Possession	49%	40%

PREMIERSHIP STANDINGS

Position (pos before)	W	D	L	F	A	Pts
17 (16) Bolton	1	5	4	8	19	8
4 (4) Birmingham	5	4	1	9	5	19

Simon Charlton in action.

Bolton Wanderers 2

STARTING LINE-UPS

Poole

Hunt   Thome   Charlton (c)   Barness

Ba   Campo   Nolan

Stelios   Pedersen
Jardel

Wallace

Shaw

Southall   Smith (c)   Hessenthaler

Hills   Cox   Hope   Ashby   Nosworthy

Brown

Jaaskelainen, Vaz Te   Spiller, James
Comyn-Platt   King, Perpetuini
Gardner, Okocha.   Sidibe.

"It shows how far we have come when we can comfortably beat a very good First Division unit we actually struggled against three seasons ago."
— Sam Allardyce

Wanderers' comfortable 2-0 win against First Division Gillingham came at a price, as Emerson Thome limped off the field after 66 minutes with a hamstring injury which would sideline him for several weeks.

Stelios and Henrik Pedersen got their first goals of the season in a game Wanderers dominated without breaking too much sweat.

Sam Allardyce made six changes to the team that suffered a narrow defeat to Birmingham City in the previous match, with Mario Jardel and Ibrahim Ba both starting.

Stelios confirmed his attacking intentions for the game with a first-minute free kick which flew just over Jason Brown's bar.

Gills player-boss Andy Hessenthaler went close on five minutes when he fired wide past Kevin Poole after being set up by John Hills.

Ivan Campo hit a 20-yarder over Brown's bar a minute later, while Thome followed up with a left-footer which took a deflection.

Former Arsenal and Millwall striker Paul Shaw put the ball in the net for the visitors on 21 minutes with a fantastic diving header, but his effort was ruled out for offside.

Stelios scored his first goal for the club in bizarre fashion four minutes later.

The move began with Thome appearing to over-hit his pass for Nicky Hunt on the right, but the right-back stretched out a leg to keep the ball in play and whipped in a cross which took a wicked deflection off defender Hills. Brown came racing off his line in an attempt to catch the ball, but he misjudged the spin, the ball looped over him, and there was the Greek winger to impudently nod the ball into an unguarded net.

Jardel fired in a rasper of a shot four minutes later as Wanderers looked to increase their lead.

Pedersen, who was joint-top scorer last season with seven goals, then opened his account with a well-struck left-footer after being set up by Kevin Nolan.

Poole then made a great save to deny Nyron Nosworthy a consolation score for the lowly First Division side.

And Jardel missed a glorious opportunity to make it 3-0 in the final minutes when he turned Hunt's low delivery over the bar from just two yards out.

0 Gillingham

KICK OFF

25 ⊙ Stelios (Open Play)

HALF TIME 1-0

46 ⇄ Hessenthaler (Off) King (On)

50 ⇄ Stelios (Off) Gardner (On)

66 ⇄ Ba (Off) Okocha (On)

66 ⊙ Pedersen (Open Play)

68 ⇄ Shaw (Off) Sidibe (On)

73 ⇄ King (Off) James (On)

FULL TIME 2-0

STATISTICS

8	Shots On Target	3
11	Shots Off Target	5
0	Hit Woodwork	0
1	Caught Offside	5
9	Corners	6
9	Fouls	9

Kevin Nolan congratulates Henrik Pedersen.

Stelios opens the scoring for Bolton.

Tottenham Hotspur 0

FIXTURE INFORMATION

Premiership
Saturday 1st November 2003
Venue: **White Hart Lane**
Attendance: **35,191**
Referee: **U.D.Rennie**

PREMIERSHIP FIXTURE HISTORY

	Played:5 Draws:1	Wins ⚽	⬜	⬛
Tottenham Hotspur	3	9	6	0
Bolton Wanderers	1	6	10	0

STARTING LINE-UPS

🔹 Postiga, Blondel,
Mabizela, Burch,
Bunjevcevic.

⬛ Pedersen, Ba,
Barness, Jardel,
Poole.

Kevin Nolan's fourth goal of the season powered Wanderers to their first victory at White Hart Lane in 44 years.

Nolan, enjoying a fine goalscoring run since being converted from a midfield position to a more attacking role, capitalised on Wanderers' dominance to fire his side in front after 73 minutes and become the club's top scorer in the process.

The win was no more than Wanderers deserved, with Jay-Jay Okocha turning in a true captain's performance to inspire his team-mates.

Spurs had their best moments of the half during the early stages, highlighted by a well-directed drive from Gus Poyet in the 15th minute which forced Jussi Jaaskelainen into a smart save.

Three minutes later, Kevin Nolan registered Wanderers' first effort of note with a low shot that was saved by Kasey Keller.

Okocha was involved in most of the attacking action, and he almost gave the visitors an early lead after 19 minutes when his left-footed strike from 20 yards rattled Keller's bar. He followed that up three minutes later with a curling free kick, again from 20 yards, which flew just over the bar.

Spurs were on the back foot now, a far cry from the side recently revitalised under caretaker manager David Pleat.

Wanderers had another great chance just before the break when Ricardo Gardner crossed a perfect ball for Stelios, but the Greek winger couldn't time his volley well enough to trouble Keller.

Pleat tried to shake things up at the half, inserting Portuguese strike Helder Postiga for Poyet.

Okocha was thwarted by the woodwork once again when his 57th-minute free kick deflected off Per Frandsen and hit Keller's bar.

Wanderers survived a penalty appeal when Paul Konchesky appeared to have been nudged off the ball by Nicky Hunt, but the on-loan Charlton star stayed on his feet.

Unbelievably, Wanderers then hit the bar for a third time, as Stelios's effort glanced off Keller's fingertips and onto the woodwork.

But Wanderers got their just rewards on 73 minutes, as Nolan pounced on Keller's parry of a fierce Okocha strike and guided the ball home – much to the delight of the travelling Wanderers fans.

And there was more to come from man-of-the-match Okocha, who hit the crossbar yet again with an 80th-minute free kick.

1 Bolton Wanderers

Kevin Nolan and Kevin Davies celebrate the winner.

"On chances created and shots on goal, we dominated the game." – Sam Allardyce

Bolton Wanderers 0

FIXTURE INFORMATION

Premiership
Saturday 8th November 2003
Venue: **Reebok Stadium**
Attendance: **25,619**
Referee: **H.M.Webb**

PREMIERSHIP FIXTURE HISTORY

Played:**5** Draws:**3**	Wins	⚽	⬜	⬛
Bolton Wanderers	0	1	8	0
Southampton	2	3	7	2

STARTING LINE-UPS

Jaaskelainen

Hunt   N'Gotty   Charlton   Gardner

Frandsen   Campo   Okocha (c)

Nolan   Davies   Stelios

Beattie   Phillips

Marsden   Delap   A.Svensson   Telfer

Le Saux   M.Svensson   Lundekvam   Dodd (c)

Niemi

Ba, Pedersen,
Barness, Jardel,
Poole.

Prutton, Griffit,
Ormerod, Jones,
Higginbotham.

PREMIERSHIP MILESTONES

This game marked 75th Premiership appearances for Ricardo Gardner and Simon Charlton.

Antti Niemi once again frustrated Wanderers with several world-class saves in a scoreless encounter at the Reebok Stadium.

The Finnish international's impressive display matched his performance in last season's home encounter between the two sides, which also ended a draw.

Jay-Jay Okocha played another inspired game to lead his side's attack.

He created Wanderers' first chance when he picked up the ball in his own half and hit a crossfield pass to Kevin Davies, who knocked it down for an in-form Kevin Nolan to fire a rising drive over the bar.

Okocha then shot a low effort at Niemi after Per Frandsen had impudently dispossessed Graeme Le Saux.

James Beattie registered Saints' first noteworthy effort on 16 minutes, when his powerful 30-yard free kick flew narrowly wide.

Seconds later, Niemi produced the first of his stunning saves, tipping over an Okocha free kick which was heading straight for the top corner.

Niemi then made two easy saves, as Wanderers were forced to shoot from distance.

First, Davies chipped the ball into the arms of his former team-mate, and then Niemi dived to keep out Frandsen's shot.

Saints had a glorious opportunity to take the lead on the brink of half time, but Simon Charlton managed to deflect Paul Telfer's drive away for a corner.

Ivan Campo tried his luck minutes after the restart, but Niemi safely gathered.

Okocha produced another moment of magic just before the hour mark when he cut in from the right and fired a powerful effort which brought out the best in Niemi.

Wanderers looked to have finally found a way past the Saints keeper when Stelios got a touch to a Frandsen effort and slotted the ball home after 57 minutes. But the Greek's celebration was quickly cut short by the linesman's offside flag.

Niemi then fumbled a powerful Campo drive, but he had enough time to regain the ball before substitute Henrik Pedersen could pounce.

Fellow sub Mario Jardel missed a great opportunity to break the deadlock, stabbing the ball over the bar with the outside of his right foot.

Jardel was involved in an off the ball spat with Michael Svensson five minutes from time. Both players were booked, but as it was the Swede's second, he was dismissed.

Despite their numerical advantage, Wanderers still couldn't find a way through, as Southampton defended stoutly to preserve the draw.

0 Southampton

Jay-Jay Okocha springs an attack.

"It was disappointing that we didn't clinch another victory. " — Sam Allardyce

STATISTICS

This Season	This Match		This Season	This Match
68	10	Shots On Target	2	62
86	8	Shots Off Target	2	62
6	0	Hit Woodwork	0	6
32	2	Caught Offside	2	43
81	8	Corners	6	71
165	11	Fouls	15	166
43%	49%	Possession	51%	45%

PREMIERSHIP STANDINGS

Position (pos before)	W	D	L	F	A	Pts
14 (15) Bolton	2	6	4	9	19	12
9 (10) Southampton	4	5	3	10	7	17

 # Leeds United 0

FIXTURE INFORMATION

Premiership
Saturday 22nd November 2003
Venue: **Elland Road**
Attendance: **36,558**
Referee: **G.Poll**

PREMIERSHIP FIXTURE HISTORY

Played:5 Draws:1	Wins	🏆	⬜	⬛
Leeds United	1	4	11	0
Bolton Wanderers	3	7	6	0

STARTING LINE-UPS

Robinson

Camara · Duberry · Radebe (c) · Harte

Milner · Morris · Batty · Seth Johnson

Sakho · Viduka

Stelios · Davies · Nolan

Okocha (c) · Campo · Frandsen

Gardner · Charlton · N'Gotty · Hunt

Jaaskelainen

🧤 Chapuis, Olembe, Barmby, Domi, Carson.

👕 Pedersen, Barness, Djorkaeff, Jardel, Poole.

PREMIERSHIP MILESTONES

Stelios Giannakopoulos scored his first Premiership goal.

Goals from Kevin Davies and Stelios gave Wanderers their second successive away victory as they consigned Leeds United to their sixth consecutive defeat.

The pair struck their goals in a productive minute for Wanderers early in the first half, effectively putting the game beyond reach.

Sam Allardyce started his 200th game in charge with the same line-up that drew 0-0 against Southampton a fortnight before.

Youri Djorkaeff had recovered from a problematic calf injury to earn himself a place on the bench after a five-game absence.

Eddie Gray, newly installed as caretaker manager following the sacking of Peter Reid, welcomed Australian international Mark Viduka back to the starting line-up.

The hosts started the brighter of the two sides, but failed to capitalise on their early dominance as Wanderers fired those two early goals.

The first began with a surging run down the left by Ricardo Gardner, who eventually fired the ball into the Leeds box. Michael Duberry cleared, but only as far as Davies, who was lurking near the penalty spot. The Wanderers striker had plenty of time to place his shot past Paul Robinson to give the visitors an early lead on 16 minutes.

Wanderers then doubled their advantage less than a minute later, as Davies crossed for Stelios to nab his first Premiership goal for the club.

Robinson came to the rescue for Leeds three minutes later when he made a fine save to deny Per Frandsen after the Dane had been teed up by Stelios.

Bruno N'Gotty went close just after the half-hour mark, rising unchallenged to meet Stelios's lofted ball.

Viduka was unfortunate not to pull a goal back for Leeds five minutes after the restart.

The Wanderers defence were deep as they tried to play the striker offside, but the linesman's flag wasn't forthcoming and Jussi Jaaskelainen had to race off his line to block the Aussie's effort.

The Finn made another fine save off Lamine Sahko five minutes later, after Kevin Nolan had lost possession deep inside his own half.

The home side had Robinson to thank once again on 64 minutes when he turned Frandsen's 30-yard effort away for a corner.

Leeds didn't really threaten for the rest of the match, as the Wanderers defence stood firm to claim their third successive Premiership clean sheet to go with those precious three points.

2 Bolton Wanderers

Kevin Davies congratulates Stelios on his goal.

"I celebrated the goal like crazy because for many weeks I couldn't score, so I felt a little pressure." – Stelios

EVENT LINE

16 ⊙ Davies (Open Play)

17 ⊙ Stelios (Open Play)

HALF TIME 0-2

46 ⇄ Batty (Off) Chapuis (On)

67 ☐ Sakho (Foul)

74 ⇄ **Nolan (Off) Pedersen (On)**

77 ⇄ Johnson (Off) Barmby (On)

77 ⇄ Morris (Off) Olembe (On)

FULL TIME 0-2

STATISTICS

This Season	This Match		This Season	This Match
48	7	Shots On Target	3	71
61	2	Shots Off Target	6	92
1	0	Hit Woodwork	0	6
39	4	Caught Offside	2	34
54	8	Corners	2	83
206	15	Fouls	12	177
43%	49%	Possession	51%	43%

PREMIERSHIP STANDINGS

Position (pos before)	W	D	L	F	A	Pts
20 (20) Leeds	2	2	9	11	33	8
13 (14) Bolton	3	6	4	11	19	15

Bolton Wanderers 2

FIXTURE INFORMATION

Premiership
Saturday 29th November 2003
Venue: **Reebok Stadium**
Attendance: **27,350**
Referee: **P.A.Durkin**

PREMIERSHIP FIXTURE HISTORY

	Played: 5 Draws: 3	Wins ⚽	⬜	⬛
Bolton Wanderers	1	6	8	1
Everton	1	5	6	1

STARTING LINE-UPS

Jaaskelainen

Hunt N'Gotty Charlton Gardner

Frandsen Campo Okocha (c)

Nolan Stelios

Davies

Radzinski Rooney

Kilbane Linderoth Gravesen Carsley

Unsworth Stubbs (c) Yobo Hibbert

Martyn

Djorkaeff, Thome,
Pedersen, Jardel,
Poole.

McFadden, Nyarko,
Jeffers, Naysmith,
Simonsen.

Wanderers recorded their first back-to-back Premiership victories since April as they cruised to a comfortable win against Everton.

Goals from Per Frandsen and Kevin Nolan lifted Wanderers to 10th in the Premiership, as they matched the previous week's result at Leeds.

With this victory Wanderers made it 10 points in their last four games, as they began to show signs of slowly turning their fortunes around following a sluggish start to the season.

Sam Allardyce stuck with the same 11 that had picked up a second successive away win against Leeds, electing to keep fit-again Youri Djorkaeff on the bench.

The hard-working Kevin Davies might have given Wanderers the lead as early as the second minute when he rose to meet Jay-Jay Okocha's cross from the right, but he could only nod it over the bar.

Wanderers were looking very sharp, and when Nolan sent Stelios on a run, it looked like the Greek star would hit his second goal in as many matches; but he knocked the ball agonisingly wide of the advancing Nigel Martyn.

The hosts' enterprising play was eventually rewarded with a goal in the 26th minute.

Martyn could only manage a weak punch as he attempted to clear Ivan Campo's header, and the ball fell straight to Per Frandsen, whose instant header settled into the back of the net for the Dane's first goal of the season.

Wanderers were enjoying the vast majority of possession and Everton never seemed a threat to the home defence or keeper Jussi Jaaskelainen.

Seven minutes before the break, Davies saw another header off an Okocha cross fly over the bar.

Wanderers doubled their lead less than a minute after the restart, as Nolan wrong-footed Martyn with a final touch to Djorkaeff's spectacularly acrobatic volley from just outside the Toffees box. It was the young Scouser's fifth goal of the season.

Everton were looking more and more uncomfortable, particularly as they struggled to contain the graceful Djorkaeff and Okocha.

The Wanderers defence, meanwhile, were in command, comfortably claiming their fourth successive league clean sheet.

0 Everton

Everton

Kevin Nolan tackles Thomas Gravesen

"All my mates are Everton fans, and none of them will be going out after the game – they'll all be in their beds crying!"
– Kevin Nolan

EVENT LINE

26 ⊙ Frandsen (Open Play)

30 ⇄ Stelios (Off) Djorkaeff (On)

HALF TIME 1-0

46 ⊙ Djorkaeff (Indirect Free Kick)

46 ⇄ Linderoth (Off) McFadden (On)

54 ⇄ Rooney (Off) Jeffers (On)

61 ▨ Carsley (Ung Conduct)

61 ▨ McFadden (Ung Conduct)

71 ⇄ Gravesen (Off) Nyarko (On)

FULL TIME 2-0

STATISTICS

This Season	This Match		This Season	This Match
75	4	Shots On Target	1	65
100	8	Shots Off Target	5	86
6	0	Hit Woodwork	0	4
39	5	Caught Offside	2	40
90	7	Corners	7	91
190	13	Fouls	16	184
44%	48%	Possession	52%	46%

PREMIERSHIP STANDINGS

Position (pos before)	W	D	L	F	A	Pts
10 (14) Bolton	4	6	4	13	19	18
18 (15) Everton	3	4	7	15	19	13

Liverpool 2

FIXTURE INFORMATION

Carling Cup 4th Round
Wednesday 3rd December 2003
Venue: **Anfield**
Attendance: **33,185**
Referee: **M.A.Riley**

STARTING LINE-UPS

Dudek

Otsemobor   Biscan   Traore   Riise

Diouf   Diao   Murphy (c)   Smicer

Heskey
Le Tallec

Jardel

Pedersen   Djorkaeff

Okocha (c)   Campo   Ba

Gardner   N'Gotty   Thome   Barness

Poole

Kirkland, Cheyrou   Jaaskelainen
Gerrard, Kewell   Charlton, Frandsen
Sinama-Pongolle   Nolan, Davies

"We are now in the quarter-final – it's a big achievement and we want to keep on going"
— Jay-Jay Okocha

A late penalty score by Youri Djorkaeff dumped holders Liverpool out of the Carling Cup after they had twice fought back to equalise.

The French maestro was the coolest man in Anfield as his 90th-minute spot kick cannoned in off the post to put Wanderers into the quarter-finals, after goals from Mario Jardel and Jay-Jay Okocha had been cancelled out by Danny Murphy and Vladimir Smicer.

Wanderers opened the scoring in the fourth minute, as an unchallenged Jardel rose to meet Djorkaeff's corner and head past Jerzy Dudek. It was the Brazilian's third goal in the competition.

Wanderers nearly lost the lead moments later, as Kevin Poole's low save of John Arne Riise's powerful drive fell to Smicer in front of goal; but the Czech midfielder hit it over the bar.

England striker Emile Heskey then also fired over after collecting Smicer's great cross from the left.

Henrik Pedersen missed a good opportunity to double Wanderers' lead just before the half-time whistle, steering the ball past Dudek's left post off Ibrahim Ba's cross from the right.

The hosts stepped up a gear following the restart and could have found themselves two goals to the good in the space of a minute.

First, Senegal star El-Hadji Diouf evaded the offside trap to run clear of the Wanderers' defence, but his first touch let him down and Ricardo Gardner was able to clear for a corner.

Then, Ivan Campo had to clear off his line after a Liverpool corner cut through the Wanderers defence.

On 66 minutes Liverpool got the equaliser their second-half resurgence deserved, as captain Murphy arrived at the far post to head Salif Diao's cross from the right past Poole.

Four minutes later, substitute Kevin Davies – on for Jardel – saw a looping volley fall into the grateful arms of Dudek.

The hordes of travelling Wanderers fans thought Djorkaeff had restored the lead on 75 minutes when he steered a loose ball over the line, but referee Mike Riley brought play back to award a free kick to Liverpool.

Four minutes later and the disallowed goal didn't matter, as Okocha fired a powerful free kick past Dudek for his first goal of the season.

Liverpool equalised through Smicer in the 88th minute, before Djorkaeff responded with the dramatic winner a minute later, firing home from the spot after Davies had been upended in the box.

3 Bolton Wanderers

Youri Djorkaeff celebrates the last-minute winner.

EVENT LINE

KICK OFF

4 ⚽ Jardel (Corner)

HALF TIME 0-1

59 🔄 Diouf (Off) Kewell (On)

59 🔄 Le Tallec (Off) Sinama-Pongolle (On)

62 🔄 **Jardel (Off) Davies (On)**

66 ⚽ Murphy (Open Play)

67 🔄 Traore (Off) Gerrard (On)

79 ⚽ **Okocha (Direct Free Kick)**

83 🔄 **N'Gotty (Off) Charlton (On)**

88 ⚽ Smicer (Open Play)

90 🔄 **Djorkaeff (Off) Nolan (On)**

90 ⚽ **Djorkaeff (Penalty)**

FULL TIME 2-3

STATISTICS

10	Shots On Target	5
6	Shots Off Target	6
1	Hit Woodwork	0
3	Caught Offside	3
8	Corners	3
17	Fouls	15

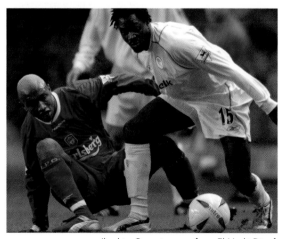

Ibrahim Ba gets away from El-Hadji Diouf.

Fulham 2

FIXTURE INFORMATION

Premiership
Saturday 6th December 2003
Venue: **Loftus Road**
Attendance: **14,393**
Referee: **A.P.D'Urso**

PREMIERSHIP FIXTURE HISTORY

	Played:**3** Draws:**0**	Wins	⚽	☐	■
Fulham		3	9	1	0
Bolton Wanderers		0	2	4	0

STARTING LINE-UPS

van der Sar

Volz Knight Melville (c) Bonnissel

Davis Legwinski Clark

Inamoto

Malbranque

Saha

Davies

Djorkaeff Nolan

Okocha (c) Campo Frandsen

Gardner Charlton N'Gotty Hunt

Jaaskelainen

Hayles, Sava,
Djetou, Goma,
Crossley.

Jardel, Ba,
Stelios, Thome,
Poole.

PREMIERSHIP MILESTONES

Kevin Davies scored his 25th
Premiership goal. **25**

Former AC Milan player Ibrahim
Ba made his Premiership debut.

Wanderers fell to their first league defeat in five games after Fulham came from behind to beat them at Loftus Road.

Sean Davis and Facundo Sava scored inside a minute to cancel out Kevin Davies' second-half opener.

Wanderers almost had a dream start just 13 seconds into the game, as Simon Charlton launched an inch-perfect pass to Davies, who flicked the ball on to Kevin Nolan. The big striker knocked a deft lob towards the Fulham goal, but keeper Edwin van der Sar raced off his line to tip the ball away for a corner.

Ricardo Gardner made a strong run on 11 minutes, evading a couple of challenges as he galloped down the left-hand side, but he could only muster a harmless shot across the face of goal.

Former Newcastle midfielder Lee Clark had the hosts' first shot after latching onto a loose ball, but he fired over Jussi Jaaskelainen's bar.

Youri Djorkaeff had a good chance to break the deadlock a minute later, but he opted for precision rather than power and couldn't find a way past Van der Sar's giant frame.

Fulham wasted a good chance on 35 minutes when Junichi Inamoto raced clear, but he blasted the ball high and wide with only Jaaskelainen to beat.

Wanderers' perseverance finally paid off eight minutes after the restart, as Ivan Campo flicked a Jay-Jay Okocha throw-in into the path of Davies, who fired the ball past Van der Sar.

Davies was presented with an even easier chance less than a minute later, but his header hit the ground and bounced over the bar.

In a crazy one-minute spell against the run of play, the hosts found themselves on level terms, and then with their noses in front.

First, homegrown youngster Davis volleyed his side back into the game after substitute Barry Hayles had charged into the box.

Then, less than a minute later, Argentine substitute Sava fired past Jaaskelainen after some more probing work from Hayles.

Sam Allardyce then inserted attacking replacements Stelios, Mario Jardel and Ibrahim Ba.

And Wanderers so nearly snatched an equaliser in the final minute of injury time, as Jardel hit the post with a header and watched the ball rebound into the arms of Van der Sar.

1 Bolton Wanderers

Nicky Hunt stays strong against Steed Malbranque.

Per Frandsen looks for space.

"The bottom-line is that we had plenty of chances but didn't take them, and we paid a very heavy price for that." — Sam Allardyce

Chelsea 1

FIXTURE INFORMATION

Premiership
Saturday 13th December 2003
Venue: **Stamford Bridge**
Attendance: **40,491**
Referee: **M.D.Messias**

PREMIERSHIP FIXTURE HISTORY

	Played: 5 Draws: 0	Wins ⚽	☐	■
Chelsea	4	12	9	0
Bolton Wanderers	1	5	10	0

STARTING LINE-UPS

Cudicini

Johnson Terry Desailly (c) Bridge

Gronkjaer Makelele Lampard Duff

Crespo Mutu

Davies

Djorkaeff Nolan

Okocha (c) Campo Frandsen

Gardner Charlton N'Gotty Hunt

Jaaskelainen

Geremi, J Cole,
Gallas, Hasselbaink,
Ambrosio.

Stelios, Pedersen,
Barness, Ba,
Poole.

Wanderers ended Chelsea's unbeaten home record as they claimed their first win at Stamford Bridge in 28 years.

Henrik Pedersen had only been on the field for three minutes when his 90th-minute cross was steered into the net by home defender John Terry to give Wanderers a deserved win.

Chelsea dominated the first-half action, though.

Their first chance came on 10 minutes, as Adrian Mutu's cross from the left fell to Hernan Crespo, but his shot on the turn was off-target.

The Argentine hitman found the back of the net three minutes later, but his effort was ruled out after he had brought the ball under control with his hand.

Mutu then went on a fantastic run after dispossessing Wanderers captain Jay-Jay Okocha, but his shot curled wide.

Chelsea's pressure finally paid off on 22 minutes, as Terry's towering header from Damien Duff's corner was headed home by Crespo.

Wanderers then went upfield and had a goal ruled out themselves.

Ivan Campo and Kevin Nolan caused confusion in the Londoners' box, and the Spaniard blasted the ball home after Carlo Cudicini appeared to spill it. But the referee spotted an infringement on the Chelsea keeper and awarded the home side a free kick instead.

Duff caused more consternation for the visitors' defence when his low, left-footed cross slid across the face of goal, but the ball eventually rolled away for a goal kick.

Six minutes before the break, Wanderers got themselves back on level terms through Bruno N'Gotty, the big Frenchman out-jumping compatriot Marcel Desailly to knock Youri Djorkaeff's free kick past Cudicini for his second goal of the campaign.

Wanderers had more possession in the first 10 minutes of the second period than they'd had in the entire first half, and their increasing confidence was epitomised in the 65th minute when substitute Stelios's clever run into the box opened space for Per Frandsen to thump a 25-yarder which Cudicini acrobatically tipped away for a corner.

Mutu's overhead kick sailed over the bar moments later, before frustrated Claudio Ranieri worked his substitutions, inserting Jimmy Floyd Hasselbaink for Jesper Gronkjaer on 70 minutes, and then Joe Cole and Geremi. But Chelsea were unable to threaten the Wanderers goal.

And then the dramatic finale, as Terry guided the ball past Cudicini in the final minute, after substitute Pedersen had made a fantastic run down the left.

2 Bolton Wanderers

Per Frandsen gets away from Frank Lampard.

STATISTICS

This Season	This Match		This Season	This Match
82	2	Shots On Target	2	83
101	4	Shots Off Target	4	110
2	0	Hit Woodwork	0	6
52	2	Caught Offside	2	45
88	7	Corners	3	95
229	17	Fouls	14	219
53%	54%	Possession	46%	43%

PREMIERSHIP STANDINGS

Position (pos before)	W	D	L	F	A	Pts
2 (1) Chelsea	11	3	2	30	12	36
10 (13) Bolton	5	6	5	16	22	21

Pedersen celebrates the winning goal

"When we play like this, we're as good as anybody." — Sam Allardyce

Bolton Wanderers 1

FIXTURE INFORMATION

Carling Cup 5th round
Tuesday 16th December 2003
Venue: **Reebok Stadium**
Attendance: **13,957**
Referee: **P.Dowd**

STARTING LINE-UPS

Poole

Gardner Charlton N'Gotty Hunt

Ba Campo Okocha (c)

Stelios Pedersen

Davies

Delgado Ormerod

Pahars Prutton Delap Telfer

Higginbotham M.Svensson Hall Dodd (c)

Niemi

Jaaskelainen   Jones, Kenton
Barness, Djorkaeff   Fernandes,
Nolan, Jardel.   Marsden, McCann.

"It's great to reach the semis." – Sam Allardyce

Henrik Pedersen struck a late extra-time winner as Wanderers progressed to the semi finals of the Carling Cup.

The Dane, whose late contribution had gifted Wanderers a shock winner against Chelsea in the previous match, latched onto substitute Anthony Barness's shot to fire past Saints keeper Antti Niemi.

Niemi had thwarted Wanderers throughout the evening with a string of world-class saves, but Pedersen stole the glory with his second goal in the competition.

Wanderers underlined their attacking intent from the start, and barely a minute had elapsed before Niemi was called upon.

The Finnish international, so often a crucial figure in Wanderers-Saints clashes, had to be at his best to block Pedersen's header off a Nicky Hunt cross. The ball was eventually cleared for a corner.

He was forced into another save just three minutes later, as Jay-Jay Okocha pounded a thunderous 25-yard free kick towards goal.

Stelios then got in on the act with two chances in the space of five seconds. Only some last-ditch defending prevented the Greek winger from breaking the deadlock.

Ibrahim Ba was the next player to fire in a shot, but his 16th-minute effort flew over the bar.

Referee Phil Dowd waved away a convincing Wanderers penalty appeal after Jason Dodd appeared to foul Pedersen inside his own box after the Dane had surged past him.

The visitors registered their first effort on target after 22 minutes when Paul Telfer drove the ball into the arms of Kevin Poole.

As the second half began, Poole did well to tip away Brett Ormerod's header from a Dodd corner. Ormerod then hit the bar after he was released by fellow striker Augustin Delgado.

The Wanderers attack then surged back into action, as Pedersen, Kevin Davies and Okocha all went close in quick succession. Hunt then went close with a drive before Okocha thundered a shot which Niemi just about got his hands to.

Substitute Youri Djorkaeff saw a goal ruled out for offside moments after coming on just before the start of extra time.

Thoughts of a penalty shootout were quickly dispelled by Pedersen's breakthrough strike in the 115th minute.

Telfer almost snatched a late equaliser, but Poole made a splendid save to tip the ball away for a corner.

0 Southampton

Henrik Pedersen takes the plaudits after his winning goal.

EVENT LINE

KICK OFF

36 ▢ Stelios (Foul)

HALF TIME 0-0

66 ⇄ Delgado (Off) Marsden (On)

69 ⇄ Pahars (Off) McCann (On)

78 ▢ Davies (Foul)

78 ⇄ Davies (Off) Jardel (On)

90 ⇄ Stelios (Off) Djorkaeff (On)

EXTRA TIME 0-0

103 ▢ Campo (Foul)

111 ⇄ Hunt (Off) Barness (On)

111 ▢ Ormerod (Dissent)

115 ⊙ Pedersen (Corner)

118 ▢ Gardner (Foul)

FULL TIME 1-0

STATISTICS

8	Shots On Target	6
10	Shots Off Target	3
0	Hit Woodwork	1
8	Caught Offside	8
10	Corners	12
19	Fouls	14

Bruno N'Gotty takes control.

Bolton Wanderers 1

Premiership
Saturday 20th December 2003
Venue: **Reebok Stadium**
Attendance: **28,003**
Referee: **G.Poll**

PREMIERSHIP FIXTURE HISTORY

Played:5 Draws:2	Wins	⚽	☐	■
Bolton Wanderers	1	4	7	1
Arsenal	2	6	8	1

STARTING LINE-UPS

Jaaskelainen

Hunt   Thome   Charlton   Gardner

Frandsen   Campo   Okocha (c)

Nolan   Djorkaeff

Davies

Henry   Bergkamp

Pires   Gilberto   Vieira (c)   Ljungberg

Clichy   Cygan   Campbell   Toure

Lehmann

Pedersen, Ba,   Parlour, Keown,
Stelios, Barness,   Edu, Kanu,
Poole.   Stack.

Super-sub Henrik Pedersen rescued a point for Wanderers after Robert Pires had threatened to steal an undeserved victory for Arsenal.

The Danish hitman had been on the field for just eight minutes when he struck a sweet volley past Jens Lehmann.

Wanderers were in attacking mood from the off, with Kevin Davies coming close to connecting with Jay-Jay Okocha's flicked-on throw-in.

Nolan then stretched to reach Davies' flick-on, but his shot lacked power and was easily gathered by Lehmann.

Thierry Henry registered the visitors' first effort on 13 minutes, a volley which flew wide of Jussi Jaaskelainen's goal.

Emerson Thome, back from a lay-off with a chest infection, showed the Brazilian in him by hitting an overhead kick on the edge of the Gunners box, but his effort lacked power and was easily cleared by Freddie Ljungberg.

Wanderers, clearly the brighter of the two sides during the early stages, had another noteworthy effort after 23 minutes when Youri Djorkaeff fired a first-time shot just over Lehmann's bar.

Dennis Bergkamp had the Gunners' best chance of the half on 29 minutes, firing high and wide after collecting Kolo Toure's inch-perfect through-ball.

Wanderers responded with their best effort of the opening period, as Nolan's clever work in the box opened space for a shot to the far post which Lehmann somehow tipped away for a corner.

Davies had another great opportunity just a minute after the restart, but he sliced his left-footed effort wide.

Pires then put the visitors ahead against the run of play, latching onto a loose ball after Jaaskelainen had parried Ljungberg's initial effort. Wanderers had cause for complaint after Bergkamp appeared to foul Ricardo Gardner in the build-up, but the ref was having none of it and Nolan was shown a yellow card for his protestations.

Djorkaeff almost responded immediately, but Lehmann saved the Frenchman's low effort.

Okocha then left the German custodian flat-footed with a well-taken free kick, only to see the ball skim off the post for a goal kick.

Pedersen then levelled after a sustained period of Wanderers pressure.

The Danish striker, whose late involvement against Chelsea had earned Wanderers a stunning victory in the capital the previous week, struck a sublime volley past Lehmann to deservedly rescue the game for the hosts.

1 Arsenal

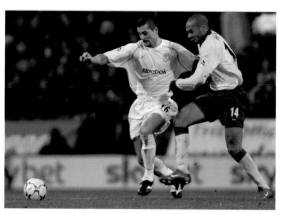

Emerson Thome takes on Thierry Henry.

EVENT LINE

HALF TIME 0-0

52 ☐ **Campo (Foul)**

54 ☐ Vieira (Foul)

57 ⊙ Pires (Open Play)

58 ☐ **Nolan (Dissent)**

64 ☐ Henry (Foul)

69 ⇄ Bergkamp (Off) Parlour (On)

75 ⇄ **Nolan (Off) Pedersen (On)**

78 ⇄ **Campo (Off) Ba (On)**

83 ⊙ **Pedersen (Indirect Free Kick)**

FULL TIME 1-1

STATISTICS

This Season	This Match		This Season	This Match
89	6	Shots On Target	4	101
118	8	Shots Off Target	4	93
7	1	Hit Woodwork	0	8
48	3	Caught Offside	2	56
103	8	Corners	1	84
232	13	Fouls	17	234
44%	45%	Possession	55%	52%

PREMIERSHIP STANDINGS

Position (pos before)	W	D	L	F	A	Pts
10 (10) Bolton	5	7	5	17	23	22
1 (1) Arsenal	11	6	0	31	12	39

Henrik Pedersen celebrates his goal with team mates

"It was one of the best goals of my career."
— Henrik Pedersen

Liverpool 3

FIXTURE INFORMATION

Premiership
Friday 26th December 2003
Venue: **Anfield**
Attendance: **42,987**
Referee: **J.T.Winter**

PREMIERSHIP FIXTURE HISTORY

	Played:5 Draws:1	Wins ⚽	☐	■
Liverpool	4	13	3	0
Bolton Wanderers	0	5	11	0

STARTING LINE-UPS

Kirkland

Otsemobor Biscan Hyypia Riise

Murphy Gerrard (c) Hamann Smicer

Kewell
Sinama-Pongolle

Davies

Djorkaeff Nolan

Okocha (c) Campo Frandsen

Gardner Charlton Thome Hunt

Jaaskelainen

Diouf, Heskey,   Stelios, Ba,
Le Tallec, Henchoz, Pedersen, Barness,
Dudek.   Poole.

Bolton conceded three goals for the first time since October 18 as they crashed away at Liverpool.

Wanderers made the short trip to Anfield searching for their first league win there since 1954.

The Merseysiders were boosted by the return of Harry Kewell after a three-week lay-off with an ankle injury, and perhaps predictably, their early attacking momentum came from their captain Steven Gerrard.

Florent Sinama-Pongolle was brought down on the edge of the Bolton penalty area in the 14th minute, but Gerrard's fizzing effort was comfortably held by Jussi Jaaskelainen.

The match then sprung into life, as John Arne Riise set off on a mazy run which saw the Norwegian international cut in from the left and fire a low, right-footed effort into the arms of Jaaskelainen.

Simon Charlton did well to block Sami Hyypia's low shot off a Gerrard corner in the 23rd minute.

Jon Otsemobor headed the ball straight to Charlton from a Youri Djorkaeff free kick, but he was unable to divert the ball goalwards.

Liverpool made Wanderers pay for that missed opportunity, as just minutes later Hyypia crashed home a thunderous header off a Danny Murphy corner.

In the 39th minute, Vladimir Smicer turned on the halfway line and ran unopposed for 30 yards before passing to Kewell, whose side-footed effort was parried by Jaaskelainen and cleared by Emerson Thome.

Wanderers should have levelled three minutes later, as Ricardo Gardner played a delightful ball into the danger area, only for Ivan Campo to head wide with the goal at his mercy.

Two minutes into the second period and Liverpool were two up, Riise breaking down the left and crossing for Sinama-Pongolle to nod home from six yards out.

Sam Allardyce then made a triple substitution, introducing Ibrahim Ba, Stelios and Henrik Pedersen for Djorkaeff, Jay-Jay Okocha and Campo in a bold attempt to stem the tide.

But just three minutes later Liverpool were another goal to the good, as Smicer headed home off Murphy's free kick from the right.

Wanderers responded with a long-range effort from Stelios which was handled by keeper Chris Kirkland.

Despite Liverpool enjoying the majority of possession, Bolton refused to give up, and with just six minutes remaining, Pedersen gave the Wanderers fans packed in behind the goal a glimmer of hope when he fired home a loose ball to reduce the arrears.

But by then, it was too little, too late.

1 Bolton Wanderers

Kevin Davies takes on Igor Biscan

Richari Gardner is chased by Liverpool's Steven Gerrard

"Our performance was unacceptable and I just hope we've got it out of our system."
— Sam Allardyce

 # Bolton Wanderers 2

FIXTURE INFORMATION

Premiership

Sunday 28th December 2003

Venue: **Reebok Stadium**

Attendance: **28,353**

Referee: **N.S.Barry**

PREMIERSHIP FIXTURE HISTORY

	Played:**3** Draws:**2**	Wins ⚽	☐	■
Bolton Wanderers	1	6	6	3
Leicester City	0	4	7	2

STARTING LINE-UPS

Jaaskelainen

Hunt　N'Gotty　Charlton　Gardner

Nolan　Campo　Okocha (c)

Stelios　　　　　　Djorkaeff

Davies

Dickov　Bent

Hignett　Izzet (c)　Davidson　Scowcroft

Thatcher　Scimeca　Heath　Curtis

Coyne

Pedersen, Thome,　Ferdinand, Brooker,
Ba, Jardel,　Stewart, Impey,
Poole.　McKinlay.

PREMIERSHIP MILESTONES

Record Premiership attendance at Reebok Stadium of 28,353

Jay-Jay Okocha and Ivan Campo made their 50th Premiership appearances.

Les Ferdinand came off the bench to earn Leicester City a last-minute point against Wanderers.

The former Spurs striker struck a typical header to stun Wanderers after Ivan Campo's second-half strike had put the hosts in front.

Wanderers were hoping to show that Friday's defeat on Merseyside was a mere blip in an otherwise strong run of form.

Sam Allardyce resisted the temptation to make wholesale changes and stuck with the creative trio of Jay-Jay Okocha, Youri Djorkaeff and Campo, despite withdrawing them five minutes after half time at Anfield.

Conditions at the Reebok were treacherous, with intermittent hailstorms engulfing the stadium.

The Foxes should have taken the lead on ten minutes when Ben Thatcher beat keeper Jussi Jaaskelainen with a thunderous left-footed free kick, but the ball smacked against the left-hand post.

Eight minutes later, Wanderers found themselves a goal behind with only themselves to blame.

With plenty of time to clear the ball after taking a pass, Jaaskelainen slipped at the moment of contact and hit a soft, low ball into the path of Campo, who failed to guide the ball any further. The ball broke to Marcus Bent, who curled it around Jaaskelainen and into the net.

Wanderers took advantage of some equally sloppy defending to grab an equaliser just after the half-hour mark, as the Foxes backline failed to clear Djorkaeff's free kick, allowing Bruno N'Gotty to ghost in at the far post to claim his third goal of the season.

Nine minutes after the restart, Campo hit his second goal of the season to put his side in front.

Djorkaeff's work on the edge of the box found Kevin Nolan, who in turn squared for Campo. The Spaniard struck a low, powerful drive that whistled past debutant Danny Coyne.

Wanderers were energised by the score and looked hungry for more goals.

Djorkaeff went close with a volley just three minutes later, but for all their perseverance, the home side were unable to add to their lead.

Wanderers' appeals for a penalty after Kevin Davies appeared to be upended in the Leicester box were then waved away by referee Neale Barry.

Henrik Pedersen came on for Stelios in the 75th minute and almost hit his fourth goal in as many games as he steered his shot a couple of yards wide.

Leicester piled on the pressure towards the end and made it count through Ferdinand.

2 Leicester City

18 ⚽ Bent (Open Play)

19 ▢ Izzet (Ung Conduct)

35 ⚽ N'Gotty (Indirect Free Kick)

45 ▢ Campo (Ung Conduct)

HALF TIME 1-1

54 ⚽ **Campo (Open Play)**

54 ▢ Thatcher (Foul)

71 ⇄ Dickov (Off) Ferdinand (On)

72 ⇄ Hignett (Off) Brooker (On)

75 ⇄ **Stelios (Off) Pedersen (On)**

79 ▢ Davidson (Foul)

84 ⇄ Bent (Off) Stewart (On)

90 ⚽ Ferdinand (Corner)

FULL TIME 2-2

Nicky Hunt plays the ball out of defence.

STATISTICS

This Season	This Match		This Season	This Match
97	6	Shots On Target	5	87
131	9	Shots Off Target	2	81
7	0	Hit Woodwork	1	8
52	2	Caught Offside	6	57
107	3	Corners	7	90
266	16	Fouls	19	294
44%	57%	Possession	43%	42%

PREMIERSHIP STANDINGS

Position (pos before)	W	D	L	F	A	Pts
12 (10) Bolton	**5**	**8**	**6**	**20**	**28**	**23**
17 (18) Leicester C	4	6	9	28	31	18

"The referee got a major decision wrong. In the end, that's proved the difference between us winning and drawing."
— Sam Allardyce

Tranmere 1

FIXTURE INFORMATION

F.A. Cup 3rd Round
Saturday 3rd January 2004
Venue: **Prenton Park**
Attendance: **10,587**
Referee: **S.G.Bennett**

STARTING LINE-UPS

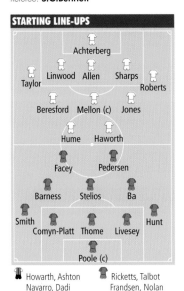

Achterberg

Linwood Allen Sharps
Taylor Roberts

Beresford Mellon (c) Jones

Hume Haworth

Facey Pedersen

Barnes Stelios Ba

Smith Hunt
Comyn-Platt Thome Livesey

Poole (c)

Howarth, Ashton
Navarro, Dadi
Hay.

Ricketts, Talbot
Frandsen, Nolan
Vaz Te.

Substitute Kevin Nolan's marvellous solo strike late in the game forced an F.A. Cup third-round replay against Second Division Tranmere Rovers.

The midfielder had only been on the field for a matter of minutes before earning Wanderers a second chance against an impressive Prenton Park outfit, who squandered a number of chances to put the tie beyond doubt.

Had goalscorer Simon Haworth been a bit more clinical, Wanderers could have suffered quite a heavy defeat.

Wanderers almost snatched an early lead through the quicksilver Delroy Facey. The Yorkshireman blazed down the right wing, but could only watch in frustration as his shot cannoned off the post before being cleared for safety.

Kevin Poole then turned away a snapshot from Haworth.

Haworth, clearly Tranmere's main scoring threat, then hit the crossbar with a 15th-minute header off Gareth Roberts's cross.

Play quickly switched to the Tranmere box and Nicky Hunt wasted a glorious chance for Wanderers when, with only John Achterberg to beat, he blasted a right-footer high over the Dutchman's bar.

Ibrahim Ba was the next Wanderer to waste a goalscoring opportunity, when his powerful strike after 27 minutes cannoned off Bolton-born defender Graham Allen for a corner.

Dangerman Haworth then watched Poole make an athletic save to thwart another good chance on the counter-attack.

Tranmere looked more fluent in the second half, with Haworth yet again testing Poole with a close-range effort just after the restart.

And the hosts soon took a deserved lead, as Haworth fired Mickey Mellon's rebound past Poole on 51 minutes.

Academy hotshot Ricardo Vaz Te came off the bench and almost equalised with his first touch in senior football. He leaped above everybody to get a head on Stelios's free kick, only to see Achterberg tip the ball away for a corner.

Allen then went close for the hosts, before Poole made another fine save to deny Haworth for the umpteenth time.

Canadian Iain Hume had a tremendous opportunity to double his side's lead when he found himself one-on-one with Poole, but Wanderers' veteran keeper made a stunning save to deny the youngster.

And then came Nolan's tremendous strike, as he charged upfield and glanced past several challenges before expertly curling a right-footer past Achterberg.

"Pooley made some fantastic saves, and Kevin Nolan took full advantage of Tranmere not capitalising on their opportunities."

— Sam Allardyce

1 Bolton Wanderers

Kevin Nolan makes sure Bolton make it into the 4th round draw.

EVENT LINE

KICK OFF

HALF TIME 0-0

46 ⇄ **Hunt (Off) Frandsen (On)**

51 ⚽ Haworth (Open Play)

53 ▢ Jones (Ung Conduct)

55 ⇄ **Smith (Off) Vaz Te (On)**

69 ⇄ **Ba (Off) Nolan (On)**

71 ⇄ Sharps (Off) Navarro (On)

76 ▢ Roberts (Foul)

78 ⚽ **Nolan (Open Play)**

80 ▢ Linwood (Foul)

85 ⇄ Hume (Off) Dadi (On)

FULL TIME 1-1

STATISTICS

13	Shots On Target	8
3	Shots Off Target	1
1	Hit Woodwork	1
2	Caught Offside	4
8	Corners	7
18	Fouls	10

Danny Livesey tackles David Beresford.

Bolton Wanderers 1

FIXTURE INFORMATION

Premiership
Wednesday 7th January 2004
Venue: **Reebok Stadium**
Attendance: **27,668**
Referee: **D.J.Gallagher**

PREMIERSHIP FIXTURE HISTORY

Played:**5** Draws:**2**	Wins	⚽	⬜	⬛
Bolton Wanderers	0	2	5	1
Manchester United	3	13	6	0

STARTING LINE-UPS

Jaaskelainen
Hunt   N'Gotty   Charlton   Gardner
Frandsen   Campo   Okocha (c)
Nolan   Djorkaeff
Davies

Giggs   van Nistelrooy
Scholes   P.Neville   Keane (c)   Fletcher
O'Shea   Silvestre   Ferdinand   G.Neville
Howard

Thome, Moreno,
Ba, Poole,
Stelios.

Butt, Fortune,
Carroll, Kleberson,
Forlan.

PREMIERSHIP MILESTONES

On-loan striker Javi Moreno made his Premiership debut.

Gary Neville's own-goal offered Wanderers a late ray of hope, but they couldn't overcome first-half goals from Paul Scholes and Ruud van Nistelrooy, as Manchester United consolidated their position at the top of the Premiership.

Wanderers fought hard throughout, and but for some heroic saves from American international Tim Howard, could have come away from the game with three points in the bag.

The visitors attacked from the off, and Simon Charlton had to make a saving tackle as early as the third minute, as van Nistelrooy evaded the Wanderers' offside trap.

Wanderers suffered a blow after 18 minutes when Ricardo Gardner suffered an injury that required him to be carried off on a stretcher. Emerson Thome came on to replace him, with Charlton making the switch to left-back.

Almost immediately, Per Frandsen forced Howard into a diving save with a wind-assisted swerving effort.

Jay-Jay Okocha, amazingly yet to score in the league this season, then went on a surging run and unleashed a wonderful effort which Howard just managed to tip over.

United took the lead after 24 minutes, as Scholes latched onto the loose ball from a Ryan Giggs shot and poked it past Jussi Jaaskelainen.

Four minutes later, Frandsen received Youri Djorkaeff's free kick and hit a dipping strike just over Howard's bar.

United doubled their lead six minutes before the break, as top scorer van Nistelrooy headed home Giggs's left-wing cross.

Wanderers might have got one back just a couple of minutes later, but Kevin Nolan couldn't get to Howard's spill of an Ivan Campo drive.

Seconds after the restart, Jaaskelainen was forced into parrying Roy Keane's piledriver.

Despite the arduous task of clawing back a two-goal deficit, Wanderers were playing with a fair degree of confidence.

With time running out, Wanderers were still trying their utmost to get back into the match, and it took a stunning save from Howard to deny Okocha's powerful strike towards the top corner.

Then, with a minute remaining, Okocha delivered a fantastic cross from the right touchline. Neville, under intense pressure from Djorkaeff, planted the ball past his own keeper to set up an intense finale.

Jaaskelainen charged up the field on several occasions to join the attack, and substitute Ibrahim Ba squandered a great opportunity to hit an injury-time equaliser when he skied the ball over the United goal.

2 Manchester United

Youri Djorkaeff grabbed a last-gasp goal for Wanderers.

EVENT LINE

18 ⮂ **Gardner (Off) Thome (On)**

24 ⊙ Scholes (Open Play)

39 ⊙ **van Nistelrooy (Open Play)**

HALF TIME 0-2

62 ▯ **Hunt (Foul)**

64 ⮂ **Nolan (Off) Moreno (On)**

82 ⮂ **Campo (Off) Ba (On)**

82 ⮂ Keane (Off) Butt (On)

84 ▯ **Frandsen (Foul)**

84 ⮂ Giggs (Off) Fortune (On)

89 ⊙ **Djorkaeff (Open Play)**

FULL TIME 1-2

STATISTICS

This Season	This Match		This Season	This Match
104	7	Shots On Target	7	110
141	10	Shots Off Target	4	102
7	0	Hit Woodwork	0	7
55	3	Caught Offside	2	81
117	10	Corners	5	104
274	8	Fouls	11	223
44%	50%	Possession	50%	52%

PREMIERSHIP STANDINGS

Position (pos before)	W	D	L	F	A	Pts
13 (12) Bolton	5	8	7	21	30	23
1 (1) Man Utd	16	1	3	40	14	49

"If we'd played in the first half like we did in the second, then it might have been a different story." — Kevin Davies

Blackburn Rovers 3

Wanderers overcame a two-goal deficit to claim their first top-flight league victory at Ewood Park in over 40 years.

Kevin Nolan opened the scoring with just 14 seconds on the clock.

After Wanderers kicked off, former Rovers striker Kevin Davies dispossessed centre-back Martin Taylor with a powerful challenge. The ball fell to Nolan, who placed a well-executed shot beyond Brad Friedel for his sixth goal of the season.

Rovers responded just a couple of minutes later, as Vratislav Gresko rampaged down the left wing and fired a left-footer beyond the despairing reach of Jussi Jaaskelainen.

On 15 minutes, Emerson Thome's header from Youri Djorkaeff's corner breached the Rovers defence, but Friedel went low to make a strong save.

On 21 minutes, one of Andy Cole's legs appeared to connect with Nicky Hunt's face, as the Wanderers youngster guided the ball out for a corner. Hunt was left clutching his face and writhing around in agony, whilst Cole escaped with a caution.

Three minutes later, with Hunt still off the pitch receiving treatment, Cole set up Dwight Yorke for Rovers' second goal.

Cole then turned goalscorer, when his attempted lob over Jaaskelainen helped in by the Finnish keeper's hand as Rovers took a commanding 3-1 lead.

Wanderers countered three minutes before the interval, as Djorkaeff broke down the left and then towards the goal, before impudently chipping the advancing Friedel.

Wanderers should have restored parity six minutes after the restart.

Djorkaeff latched onto Ivan Campo's long-range pass into the Rovers box and knocked it on for Stelios. But with time to place his effort, the Greek winger fired straight at Friedel.

Wanderers' perseverance was eventually rewarded on 73 minutes, as Hunt floated a cross into the box to an unmarked Stelios, who had the easiest of tasks to place the ball past Friedel and tie it up at 3-3.

Davies wasted a golden opportunity to put Wanderers ahead moments later, when his free header went the wrong side of the post.

The striker needn't have worried, however, as two minutes later Nolan put Wanderers ahead for the second time as he spun in front of goal and scrambled the ball home.

Ten minutes before time, Javi Moreno squandered a chance to increase the visitors' lead, when his left-footed strike flew across the face of goal.

Wanderers wasted further goalscoring opportunities, but hung on to claim a truly remarkable victory.

4 Bolton Wanderers

Kevin Nolan gave Wanderers an early lead.

Ivan Campo turns away from Jonathan Douglas.

"It was an unbelievable fightback by the players." — Sam Allardyce

Bolton Wanderers Official Yearbook 2004-2005   **65**

EVENT LINE

1 ⚽	**Nolan (Open Play)**
3 ⚽	Gresko (Open Play)
22 ▢	Cole (Foul)
24 ⚽	Yorke (Open Play)
31 ⮂	**Frandsen (Off) Stelios (On)**
34 ⚽	Cole (Open Play)
43 ⚽	**Djorkaeff (Open Play)**
HALF TIME 3-2	
50 ▢	**Nolan (Foul)**
55 ▢	Gresko (Foul)
57 ▢	**Hunt (Foul)**
64 ⮂	Gallagher (Off) Baggio (On)
69 ⮂	**Charlton (Off) Moreno (On)**
73 ⚽	**Stelios (Open Play)**
74 ⮂	Douglas (Off) Danns (On)
78 ⚽	**Nolan (Corner)**
83 ⮂	Neill (Off) Jansen (On)
84 ▢	**Davies (Foul)**
86 ⮂	**Davies (Off) Pedersen (On)**
FULL TIME 3-4	

STATISTICS

This Season	This Match		This Season	This Match
103	3	Shots On Target	8	112
131	5	Shots Off Target	9	150
4	0	Hit Woodwork	0	7
85	1	Caught Offside	3	58
136	4	Corners	7	124
323	15	Fouls	13	287
49%	48%	Possession	52%	45%

PREMIERSHIP STANDINGS

Position (pos before)	W	D	L	F	A	Pts
16 (15) Blackburn	6	4	11	31	35	22
11 (13) Bolton	**6**	**8**	**7**	**25**	**33**	**26**

Bolton Wanderers 1

FIXTURE INFORMATION

F.A. Cup 3rd Round Replay
Tuesday 13th January 2004
Venue: **Reebok Stadium**
Attendance: **8,759**
Referee: **H.M.Webb**

STARTING LINE-UPS

Poole

Barness Livesey Comyn-Platt Smith

Stelios Vaz Te Frandsen

Facey Jardel Pedersen

Dadi

Hume

Harrison Mellon (c) Beresford

Roberts Sharps Allen Jones G.Taylor

Achterberg

Shakes,Taylor,   Hay, Navarro,
Nolan, Ricketts,   Connelly, Howarth,
Talbot.   Linwood.

"When you don't take your chances, you pay the penalty no matter what level you're playing at."
— Sam Allardyce

Second division Tranmere Rovers edged out a below-strength Wanderers in extra time, thanks to a great individual effort from Canadian international Iain Hume.

The stocky winger hit a sublime shot from 18 yards just a minute into extra time to set up a fourth-round away tie against Luton Town.

Sam Allardyce made 10 changes to the side that beat Blackburn Rovers at the weekend, with Danish midfielder Per Frandsen the only one to retain his starting role.

Despite missing the talents of Jay-Jay Okocha, Youri Djorkaeff and Ivan Campo, Wanderers made a bright start, with fullback Anthony Barness firing just wide in the second minute.

Academy youngster Ricardo Vaz Te then picked out Mario Jardel, but the former Golden Boot winner could only muster a tame effort.

The visitors then started to find their rhythm and came close to opening the scoring in the 16th minute, when Eugene Dadi headed tGareth Roberts' cross down, to create a chance for Danny Harrison.

Henrik Pedersen provided an immediate response, but his powerful strike deflected off John Achterberg's post.

During the interval, Kevin Nolan, the two-goal hero at Blackburn, replaced Jardel.

Tranmere looked a different unit in the second period, managing a far greater share of possession.

Dadi had a good chance in the 53rd minute when Ryan Taylor picked him out with a superb long pass, but his touch let him down.

Barness had another good effort five minutes later, but his strike sailed over the bar.

With time ticking away, Allardyce brought on Cleveland Taylor to inject some pace into the attack.

Dadi put the visitors ahead in the 82nd minute when he capitalised on some hesitancy in defence to poke the ball past Kevin Poole.

Ricky Shakes made his first senior appearance for the club when he replaced Stelios with four minutes remaining.

And the London-born youngster sent the game into extra time when his deflected shot flew past Achterberg.

Hume's wonder-goal a minute into extra time proved decisive, though Pedersen's misplaced header late in the second period should have sent the game into a penalty shootout.

2 Tranmere

Ricardo Vaz Te on the ball.

Jeff Smith cuts in between Ryan Taylor and Alex Navarro.

EVENT LINE

KICK OFF

45 ☐ Jones (Foul)

HALF TIME 0-0

46 ⮂ Jardel (Off) Nolan (On)

79 ⮂ Facey (Off) Taylor (On)

82 ⊙ Dadi (Open Play)

86 ⮂ Stelios (Off) Shakes (On)

90 ⊙ Shakes (Indirect Free Kick)

EXTRA TIME 1-1

91 ⊙ Hume (Open Play)

97 ⮂ Beresford (Off) Hay (On)

101 ☐ Taylor (Foul)

107 ⮂ Hume (Off) Navarro (On)

110 ☐ Sharps (Foul)

112 ☐ Nolan (Dissent)

115 ☐ Taylor (Ung Conduct)

FULL TIME 1-2

STATISTICS

8	Shots On Target	4
7	Shots Off Target	7
1	Hit Woodwork	0
3	Caught Offside	6
9	Corners	5
12	Fouls	17

Bolton Wanderers 1

FIXTURE INFORMATION

Premiership
Saturday 17th January 2004
Venue: **Reebok Stadium**
Attendance: **26,558**
Referee: **P.Dowd**

PREMIERSHIP FIXTURE HISTORY

	Played	Draws	Wins ⚽	☐	■
	Played:**1**	Draws:**0**			
Bolton Wanderers	1	1	1	0	
Portsmouth	0	0	1	1	

STARTING LINE-UPS

Jaaskelainen
Hunt   Thome   N'Gotty   Barness
Nolan   Campo   Okocha (c)
Moreno   Djorkaeff
Davies

Yakubu   Sheringham (c)
Berkovic
Berger   Smertin
Hughes
Stefanovic   De Zeeuw   Pasanen   Primus
Hislop

Ba, Pedersen,
Stelios, Poole,
Charlton.

Taylor, Harper,
Wapenaar, Pulis,
Robinson.

PREMIERSHIP MILESTONES

Kevin Davies made his 150th Premiership appearance.

Kevin Davies' sixth goal of the season was the perfect reward for a tireless performance as he helped Wanderers to register their second successive Premiership win.

His first goal in six weeks – a close-range effort in the 53rd minute which slipped past keeper Shaka Hislop – gave Wanderers only their third Premiership home victory of the season.

Wanderers made 10 changes to the side that were knocked out of the F.A. Cup against Tranmere in midweek. Anthony Barness, who was all set to join West Ham on loan a few days ago, retained his place.

Javi Moreno, making his first start in a Wanderers shirt, went close to opening the scoring in the sixth minute when he struck Youri Djorkaeff's pass narrowly wide.

The duo combined again just three minutes later, this time Moreno heading the ball across goal.

Captain Jay-Jay Okocha then hit an effort wide after Djorkaeff squared a free kick to him.

Wanderers enjoyed plenty of possession, but just lacked the clinical final ball.

The visitors registered their first chance on 26 minutes when former Barnsley and Wigan Athletic central defender Arjan De Zeeuw met Alexi Smertin's cross, but the Dutchman headed a tame effort into the grateful hands of Jussi Jaaskelainen.

Hislop then fumbled an Ivan Campo volley, but the ball was cleared before Djorkaeff could reach it.

Hislop was on hand to turn away a powerful effort from Djorkaeff two minutes into the second period.

But a misjudgment by the Trinidadian keeper then led to the opening score, as Davies slipped Nicky Hunt's cross underneath him.

Five minutes later, African Cup of Nations-bound Yakubu Aiyegbeni was unlucky not to restore parity, as he spun past Emerson Thome and struck the post with a powerful effort.

Hislop then made a splendid save to deny Djorkaeff from close range after the Frenchman had received Hunt's exquisite chip.

Jaaskelainen was called into action in the 75th minute as he parried Smertin's strike.

The visitors failed to trouble Wanderers any further, and their push for a last-gasp point was made all the more difficult when defender Dejan Stefanovic was sent off after appearing to collide with referee Phil Dowd.

0 Portsmouth

Kevin Davies celebrates his winning goal.

Kevin Nolan holds off Richard Hughes.

"It was a huge victory for us, and one we worked very hard for." — Sam Allardyce

EVENT LINE

HALF TIME 0-0

53 ⊙ Davies (Open Play)

58 ▢ Hughes (Foul)

59 ▢ Okocha (Ung Conduct)

62 ⇄ Moreno (Off) Ba (On)

77 ⇄ Hughes (Off) Taylor (On)

77 ⇄ Primus (Off) Harper (On)

84 ⇄ Djorkaeff (Off) Pedersen (On)

90 ⇄ Okocha (Off) Stelios (On)

90 ▢ Stefanovic (Dissent)

FULL TIME 1-0

STATISTICS

This Season	This Match		This Season	This Match
117	5	Shots On Target	2	87
156	6	Shots Off Target	5	115
7	0	Hit Woodwork	0	3
59	1	Caught Offside	6	74
126	2	Corners	2	107
297	10	Fouls	15	361
45%	51%	Possession	49%	47%

PREMIERSHIP STANDINGS

Position (pos before)	W	D	L	F	A	Pts
10 (11) Bolton	**7**	**8**	**7**	**26**	**33**	**29**
17 (17) Portsmouth	6	4	12	25	33	22

Bolton Wanderers 5

FIXTURE INFORMATION

Carling Cup Semi Final 1st Leg
Wednesday 21st January 2004
Venue: **Reebok Stadium**
Attendance: **16,302**
Referee: **P.A.Durkin**

STARTING LINE-UPS

Jaaskelainen

Hunt   Thome   N'Gotty   Barness

Nolan   Campo   Okocha

Stelios   Djorkaeff

Davies

Angel   Vassell

Barry   Whittingham   McCann   Hendrie

Samuel   Dublin   Mellberg   Delaney

Sorensen

Poole, Charlton   Jones, Kenton
Ba, Moreno   Fernandes,
Pedersen   Marsden, McCann.

"If you can tell me about or show me a better goal than Jay-Jay's free kick, I simply won't believe it."
— Sam Allardyce

Jay-Jay Okocha gave Wanderers the perfect leaving present before embarking on his African Cup of Nations adventure by firing two stunning goals to help his side take a three-goal advantage to Villa Park for the second leg of their Carling Cup semi-final clash.

The Nigerian playmaker scored Wanderers' first and fifth goals in his final game for about a month.

Wanderers had stunned the Reebok Stadium crowd with three goals inside 17 minutes, only for Juan Pablo Angel to hit a brace to bring his side back into contention.

But two second-half goals from the hosts ensured Sam Allardyce's men were in the driving seat for a trip to Cardiff.

It took crowd favourite Okocha just two minutes to lift everybody off their seats.

Kevin Nolan was upended after latching onto a brilliant headed flick-on by Kevin Davies. Okocha stepped up to take the free kick and curled it past Thomas Sorensen.

Youri Djorkaeff was the next player to benefit from a fantastic Davies flick-on, but the Frenchman shot straight at Sorensen, who gathered the ball at the second attempt with Stelios lurking.

Nolan doubled his side's lead after nine minutes, collecting another Davies flick-on and heading upfield before placing a shot past Sorensen for his eighth goal of the campaign.

Davies also helped to set up Wanderers' third, this time heading Bruno N'Gotty's punt towards Stelios, who crashed an overhead kick past the despondent Sorensen after 17 minutes.

Angel countered for the Villans on 20 minutes, evading a number of challenges on the right before sending in a cross-shot over the head of Jussi Jaaskelainen.

The visitors were energised by the goal and started to trouble Wanderers with a succession of fast breaks.

Peter Whittingham and Lee Hendrie then combined to set up Angel's second score, albeit from an apparently offside position.

Jaaskelainen had to be at his best to deny the Villa striker a 62nd-minute hat-trick, as the Colombian rifled a free kick towards goal.

Despite Villa's pressure, Wanderers managed to move another goal ahead, as N'Gotty headed home Djorkaeff's corner in the 74th minute.

And Okocha saved the best for last, bending in a scintillating free kick from out on the left to beat Sorensen on the near post and leave the home fans dreaming of the Millennium Stadium.

2 Aston Villa

Stelios puts Wanderers 3-0 up.

EVENT LINE

2 ⚽ **Okocha (Direct Free Kick)**

9 ⚽ **Nolan (Open Play)**

17 ⚽ **Stelios (Indirect Free Kick)**

20 ⚽ Angel (Open Play)

HALF TIME 3-1

54 🔄 Mellberg (Off) Johnsen (On)

56 ⚽ Angel (Open Play)

57 🔄 Barry (Off) Hitzlsperger (On)

63 🔄 **Barness (Off) Charlton (On)**

64 ▢ McCann (Foul)

68 ▢ Vassell (Foul)

69 🔄 **Stelios (Off) Pedersen (On)**

74 ⚽ **N'Gotty (Corner)**

77 🔄 Vassell (Off) Allback (On)

80 ⚽ **Okocha (Direct Free Kick)**

84 🔄 **Djorkaeff (Off) Ba (On)**

89 ▢ Hendrie (Foul)

90 ▢ Dublin (Dissent)

FULL TIME 5-2

STATISTICS

11	Shots On Target	15
7	Shots Off Target	2
0	Hit Woodwork	0
4	Caught Offside	4
6	Corners	5
13	Fouls	21

Kevin Nolan gets away from Peter Whittingham.

Aston Villa 2

FIXTURE INFORMATION

Carling Cup Semi Final 2nd Leg
Tuesday 27th January 2004
Venue: **Villa Park**
Attendance: **36,883**
Referee: **S.G.Bennett**

STARTING LINE-UPS

Sorensen

Delaney Mellberg Dublin Samuel

Hendrie McCann Hitzlsperger Barry

Vassell Crouch

Davies

Djorkaeff Stelios

Frandsen Campo Ba

Charlton N'Gotty Thome Hunt

Jaaskelainen

Postma, Johnsen
Ridgewell, Allback
Whittingham

Poole, Barness
Vaz Te, Moreno
Pedersen

"Being in a major cup final makes me feel very proud to be part of this sport and this club" — Stelios

Wanderers overcame a late onslaught from 10-man Aston Villa to book their place in the Carling Cup final.

It was the first time in nine years that Wanderers had reached a major cup final, following their Coca Cola Cup appearance in 1995.

The game started at a very high tempo, with the hosts determined to get on the scoresheet as quickly as possible.

Darius Vassell had the Villa supporters off their seats when he latched onto Gareth Barry's knockdown in the third minute, but the England striker could only guide his shot straight into the arms of Jussi Jaaskelainen.

But Villa's fans didn't have to wait long to celebrate, as German midfielder Thomas Hitzlsperger curled a sweet left-footed free kick past Jaaskelainen to open the scoring in the 10th minute.

The goal ignited Villa, who were looking a far better unit than the one that had shown up for the first leg. Wanderers, meanwhile, were clearly rattled, struggling to find their rhythm.

Barry then had a marvellous opportunity to increase Villa's lead, but he fluffed a Jlloyd Samuel centre off the bar.

Villa's promising start took a turn for the worse on 40 minutes when Gavin McCann was shown a straight red for a terrible foul on Jaaskelainen. The Wanderers keeper was fortunate to carry on playing after such an awful challenge.

Wanderers were much improved in the second period, with the industrious Youri Djorkaeff at the centre of most of their attacking forays.

Villa might have extended their lead on 53 minutes through substitute Peter Whittingham, but the youngster spurned a marvellous chance with his left foot.

Wanderers went close as Kevin Davies broke down the right and crossed for Djorkaeff, whose header at full stretch glanced across the face of goal.

Wanderers had their best chance on 76 minutes, Davies collecting from Ivan Campo and galloping towards goal, only to fire wide while under pressure from the hard-working Olof Mellberg.

Samuel set the match up for a frantic finale when he hit Villa's second of the evening on 88 minutes, particularly when the fourth official indicated four minutes of injury time.

Villa sent everyone into the Wanderers box, but the visitors held firm until referee Steve Bennett finally blew for time.

0 Bolton Wanderers

Per Frandsen challenges Thomas Hitzlsperger.

EVENT LINE

KICK OFF

10 ⚽ Hitzlsperger (Direct Free Kick)

16 ☐ **Thome (Foul)**

26 ☐ Samuel (Foul)

27 ☐ Vassell (Foul)

30 ☐ McCann (Foul)

40 ■ McCann (Violent Conduct)

41 ☐ **Hunt (Ung Conduct)**

HALF TIME 1-0

47 ⇄ Hendrie (Off) Whittingham (On)

68 ⇄ **Charlton (Off) Barness (On)**

75 ☐ **Davies (Foul)**

78 ⇄ **Djorkaeff (Off) Pedersen (On)**

88 ⚽ Samuel (Open Play)

88 ⇄ **Frandsen (Off) Moreno (On)**

FULL TIME 2-0

STATISTICS

7	Shots On Target	3
11	Shots Off Target	4
0	Hit Woodwork	0
1	Caught Offside	1
3	Corners	3
15	Fouls	14

Sam Allardyce salutes the crowd.

⊘ Charlton Athletic 1

FIXTURE INFORMATION

Premiership
Saturday 31st January 2004
Venue: **The Valley**
Attendance: **26,249**
Referee: **A.P.D'Urso**

PREMIERSHIP FIXTURE HISTORY

	Played:3 Draws:1	Wins ⚽	☐	■
Charlton Athletic	0	3	1	0
Bolton Wanderers	**2**	**5**	**2**	**0**

STARTING LINE-UPS

Kiely

Kishishev   Fish   Perry   Hreidarsson

Holland (c)   Euell   Jensen

Johansson   Stuart

Di Canio

Davies

Pedersen   Stelios

Frandsen   Campo   Nolan

Barness   N'Gotty   Thome   Hunt

Jaaskelainen

Cole, Konchesky,
Royce, Young,
Fortune.

Ba, Moreno,
Charlton, Poole,
Vaz Te.

Top scorer Kevin Nolan hit his ninth goal of the season to help Wanderers past in-form Charlton for their third successive league victory.

Wanderers took a stunning lead after just 24 seconds, despite playing with a strong wind against them.

Kevin Davies collected Jussi Jaaskelainen's long upfield boot, beat Chris Parry's challenge and flicked the ball into the path of Henrik Pedersen, whose neat finish gave his side a dream start.

Former Wanderer Claus Jensen almost restored parity five minutes later, following good work from Paolo Di Canio on the right. With Addicks players queuing up, the Italian picked out the Dane, whose deflected effort hit the bar and went over.

Charlton were threatening an equaliser and their perseverance paid off on 12 minutes, as Jensen went on a marvellous run, enticing challenges and drawing several Wanderers defenders out of position before hitting a lofted cross to the far post which Jonatan Johansson knocked home with a diving header.

Emerson Thome had to be alert to turn away Johansson's low cross on 21 minutes. With Jason Euell lining up a free strike at goal, the Brazilian defender had no choice but to concede a corner.

Wanderers pressed forward in search of another goal, and Nolan and Davies both saw shots charged down in quick succession.

Dean Kiely prevented Wanderers from moving ahead just two minutes after the restart, getting down low to deny Nicky Hunt after the young fullback had taken a pass from Ibrahim Ba on the overlap.

Eight minutes later, Bruno N'Gotty was on hand to time a great tackle on Johansson in the danger zone.

Kiely then made the save of the game to keep the scores level, tipping away Pedersen's low right-footed curler for a corner.

Davies got a header on target just after the hour mark when he met Anthony Barness's cross, but the effort was too tame to trouble Kiely.

Charlton instantly went upfield and Carlton Cole found himself with only Jaaskelainen to beat, but the Wanderers keeper got down well to prevent the on-loan hitman from moving the hosts in front.

Nolan, returning to the side after a suspension, then put Wanderers back in front, firing past Kiely on 78 minutes after the Addicks had failed to clear Per Frandsen's corner.

2 Bolton Wanderers

Henrik Pedersen celebrates his early goal.

STATISTICS

This Season	This Match		This Season	This Match
116	6	Shots On Target	6	123
128	8	Shots Off Target	4	160
7	1	Hit Woodwork	0	7
68	1	Caught Offside	1	60
119	5	Corners	5	131
317	10	Fouls	11	308
46%	60%	Possession	40%	45%

PREMIERSHIP STANDINGS

Position (pos before)		W	D	L	F	A	Pts
4 (4)	Charlton	10	7	6	32	25	37
8 (10)	Bolton	8	8	7	28	34	32

Kevin Nolan slips past a challenge.

"We're only two points off a European place." — Sam Allardyce

Bolton Wanderers 2

FIXTURE INFORMATION

Premiership
Saturday 7th February 2004
Venue: **Reebok Stadium**
Attendance: **27,552**
Referee: **A.G.Wiley**

PREMIERSHIP FIXTURE HISTORY

		Wins	😊	⬜	⬛
Played:**5** Draws:**2**					
Bolton Wanderers	1	7	9	0	
Liverpool	2	8	9	1	

STARTING LINE-UPS

Jaaskelainen

Hunt   Thome   N'Gotty   Barness

Nolan   Campo   Frandsen

Djorkaeff (c)   Pedersen

Davies

Owen

Cheyrou

Kewell   Hamann   Gerrard (c)   Le Tallec

Carragher   Hyypia   Henchoz   Finnan

Dudek

Ba, Charlton,
Poole, Otsemobor,
Moreno.

Sinama-Pongolle,
Murphy, Biscan,
Luzi Bernardi, Riise.

PREMIERSHIP MILESTONES

Nicky Hunt scored his first Premiership goal.

Despite twice taking the lead, Wanderers marked Sam Allardyce's 100th game in charge with a point against Liverpool.

Michael Owen registered the first effort on target after two minutes, but the England striker's shot off Steven Gerrard's in-swinging free kick lacked the power to trouble Jussi Jaaskelainen.

Wanderers then opened the scoring on 11 minutes through Nicky Hunt's first goal for the club.

Henrik Pedersen latched onto Bruno N'Gotty's free kick from the centre circle and knocked the ball to Kevin Davies, whose mis-kick fell to Hunt. The right-back then struck a sweet left-footer past Jerzy Dudek.

Wanderers should have doubled their lead seven minutes later, as Hunt chipped the ball into the path of Pedersen, only for the Dane to blast his volley over the bar.

Kevin Nolan then had to leave the pitch with a cut to his face, but was only gone for a couple of minutes.

Dudek made a fine save on 23 minutes, blocking Hunt's goalbound effort after a neat one-two with Pedersen.

Per Frandsen left the field on 26 minutes with an injury and was replaced by Ibrahim Ba.

Emerson Thome made an important tackle 10 minutes later, dispossessing Harry Kewell as he skipped past the advancing Jaaskelainen and sending the ball for a corner.

The visitors wasted a good chance to equalise when Jamie Carragher fired wide, despite having time to place his shot.

As the half drew to a close, Anthony La Tallec wasted a glorious opportunity when he blazed a shot over the bar.

Liverpool eventually equalised on 51 minutes through a training-ground set-piece. Gerrard's perfect free kick from the right found the head of Sami Hyypia, who planted the ball past Jaaskelainen.

Wanderers retained their focus and were rewarded on 58 minutes, as Youri Djorkaeff latched onto a Davies knockdown and half-volleyed the ball past Dudek.

But 11 minutes later the impressive Gerrard pulled Liverpool level for the second time, as he ghosted behind Thome to volley La Tallec's cross past Jaaskelainen.

Both sides wasted good chances to win the game, Owen failing to make the most of a surging run by Gerrard and N'Gotty placing a free header wide.

Wanderers might have grabbed the points in the final minute, but Dudek made a fine save to deny Davies' volley.

2 Liverpool

Kevin Davies takes on Stephane Henchoz.

EVENT LINE

11 ⚽ Hunt (Indirect Free Kick)

14 ▯ Finnan (Foul)

26 ⇄ Frandsen (Off) Ba (On)

38 ▯ Davies (Foul)

HALF TIME 1-0

51 ⚽ Hyypia (Indirect Free Kick)

58 ⚽ Djorkaeff (Open Play)

65 ⇄ Cheyrou (Off) Sinama-Pongolle (On)

69 ⚽ Gerrard (Open Play)

79 ▯ Campo (Foul)

82 ⇄ Ba (Off) Charlton (On)

84 ⇄ Le Tallec (Off) Murphy (On)

86 ▯ Thome (Foul)

89 ▯ Kewell (Dissent)

FULL TIME 2-2

STATISTICS

This Season	This Match		This Season	This Match
127	4	Shots On Target	4	145
166	6	Shots Off Target	7	169
7	0	Hit Woodwork	0	6
63	3	Caught Offside	1	81
134	3	Corners	4	150
325	17	Fouls	17	288
44%	37%	Possession	63%	50%

PREMIERSHIP STANDINGS

Position (pos before)		W	D	L	F	A	Pts
9 (8)	Bolton	8	9	7	30	36	33
6 (5)	Liverpool	9	8	7	34	26	35

"Overall it was a magnificent performance from us and a well-deserved draw."
— Sam Allardyce

Leicester City 1

FIXTURE INFORMATION

Premiership

Tuesday 10th February 2004

Venue: **Walkers Stadium**

Attendance: **26,674**

Referee: **U.D.Rennie**

PREMIERSHIP FIXTURE HISTORY

	Played:**3** Draws:**2**	Wins ⚽	⬜	⬛
Leicester City	0	1	6	0
Bolton Wanderers	1	6	7	0

STARTING LINE-UPS

Walker

Scimeca Dabizas Taggart Thatcher

Bent Freund Nalis Guppy

Ferdinand Dickov (c)

Davies

Pedersen Djorkaeff (c)

Frandsen Campo Nolan

Charlton N'Gotty Thome Barness

Jaaskelainen

Scowcroft, Coyne, Davidson, Stewart, Sinclair.

Moreno, Poole, Otsemobor, Ba, Vaz Te.

PREMIERSHIP MILESTONES

Simon Charlton made his 200th appearance in the Premiership.

A bizarre own-goal by keeper Ian Walker helped Wanderers to a deserved point away at Leicester.

Wanderers were looking to pick up their third successive Premiership win on their travels against Micky Adams's side.

Prior to the game, a sports psychologist had volunteered his services to City in the hope of instilling greater self-confidence, and everything went according to plan when veteran striker Les Ferdinand – scorer of the Foxes' last-minute equaliser at the Reebok Stadium in December – put his side ahead on 16 minutes.

Despite being marked by two Wanderers defenders, the former Newcastle United and Spurs star managed to force a header past Jussi Jaaskelainen. Although the Finn scrambled the ball away, it was clearly over the line before it reached him. Just to make sure, Ferdinand got to the rebound and slammed it into the back of the net.

Wanderers were doing a good job of exploiting the grey area surrounding the new interpretation of the offside law, employing two players in apparently offside positions during their set-pieces.

Wanderers' equaliser came on 33 minutes, courtesy of a dreadful blunder by Walker.

It was a classic case of misdirection when Youri Djorkaeff whipped in a free kick. With Kevin Nolan and Henrik Pedersen causing consternation in the Foxes defence, Kevin Davies sneaked in to glance a touch goalwards. He turned in frustration when Walker grabbed the ball, only to be congratulated by his delighted team-mates as the ball somehow squirmed beneath the former Spurs keeper.

Leicester weren't disheartened by the unfortunate score and twice went close to regaining the lead before the half-time whistle.

First, Paul Dickov was adjudged to be offside as he slotted the ball into the net with Jaaskelainen well beaten. Lillian Nalis then saw a strong effort deflected for a corner, with the Wanderers keeper wrong-footed.

Walker partially redeemed himself when he cut out a fierce Nolan drive on the stroke of half time.

Dickov enjoyed two good chances after the restart to restore the Foxes' advantage.

He might have done better with an overhead kick which fell tamely for Jaaskelainen. He followed this up with a much stronger effort which the Wanderers keeper managed to turn away for a corner.

There was little goalmouth action from then on, and Wanderers hardly tested the shaky Walker as the game limped to a draw.

1 Bolton Wanderers

Henrik Pedersen holds off Riccardo Scimeca.

EVENT LINE

16 ⚽ Ferdinand (Open Play)

33 ⚽ **Walker (Own Goal)**

36 🔁 Bent (Off) Scowcroft (On)

36 🟨 **Nolan (Foul)**

HALF TIME 1-1

62 🟨 Thatcher (Foul)

76 🔁 Nalis (Off) Davidson (On)

80 🟨 **Davies (Foul)**

81 🔁 **Djorkaeff (Off) Moreno (On)**

83 🔁 Guppy (Off) Stewart (On)

FULL TIME 1-1

STATISTICS

This Season	This Match		This Season	This Match
116	7	Shots On Target	5	132
114	9	Shots Off Target	4	170
8	0	Hit Woodwork	1	8
77	3	Caught Offside	2	65
121	8	Corners	7	141
378	18	Fouls	12	337
43%	52%	Possession	48%	44%

PREMIERSHIP STANDINGS

Position (pos before)	W	D	L	F	A	Pts
18 (18) Leicester C	4	9	12	33	47	21
8 (9) **Bolton**	8	10	7	31	37	34

Anthony Barness escapes from Steve Guppy.

"I'm pleased with our effort. Leicester are always a difficult team to play against and it's five undefeated now." " — Sam Allardyce

Bolton Wanderers 1

FIXTURE INFORMATION

Premiership
Saturday 21st February 2004
Venue: **Reebok Stadium**
Attendance: **27,301**
Referee: **S.W.Dunn**

PREMIERSHIP FIXTURE HISTORY

	Played	Draws	Wins	☉	□	■
Bolton Wanderers	1	4	2	0		
Manchester City	1	4	10	1		

STARTING LINE-UPS

Jaaskelainen

Otsemobor Howey Charlton Barness

Nolan Campo Frandsen

Djorkaeff (c) Pedersen

Davies

Fowler Macken

McManaman Sibierski Reyna Sinclair

Tarnat Distin (c) Dunne Wright-Phillips

James

Okocha, Moreno,   Sun Jihai, Elliott,
Hunt, Poole,   Jordan, Arason,
N'Gotty.   Negouai.

Robbie Fowler's first-half brace to ended Man City's 15-match winless streak, while Wanderers lost for the first time in six league games.

The hosts made a bright start and could have taken the lead after only seven minutes when Youri Djorkaeff hit a great volley from 12 yards. But the Frenchman could only watch in frustration as England keeper David James made an outstanding save.

Simon Charlton almost scored his first goal for Wanderers on 19 minutes when he clipped the bar following some hesitant City defending.

Wanderers broke the deadlock after 22 minutes, when top scorer Kevin Nolan fired home a sublime volley, after Sylvain Distin had failed to clear Djorkaeff's free kick. It was the midfielder's 10th goal of the season.

Just a minute later and Wanderers should have been two up, as Henrik Pedersen was released by Ivan Campo, only to fire the ball across the face of goal.

Jussi Jaaskelainen denied City a minute later, tipping Jonathan Macken's shot away for a corner.

Fowler equalised on 27 minutes, as he took advantage of some slack Wanderers defending to move into an open position and head home Michael Tarnat's corner.

Four minutes later Fowler notched his and City's second.

James punted a huge clearance upfield and the ball bounced twice before reaching Fowler, who still had plenty of work to do before unleashing a spectacular right-footer past Jaaskelainen.

City were now playing with plenty of confidence, attacking the Wanderers goal as they worked to put the game beyond reach.

Jaaskelainen kept things close with an important save from Trevor Sinclair's shot.

Wanderers won a free kick in a good position four minutes before the break after Ivan Campo was brought down by his former Real Madrid team-mate Steve McManaman. But Djorkaeff fired straight into the arms of a grateful James.

City found themselves further in front just five minutes after the restart, when Charlton turned McManaman's cross past his own keeper.

Jaaskelainen kept the visitors in sight with a crucial save off Antoine Sibierski's header.

Sam Allardyce then made three substitutions, inserting Jay-Jay Okocha, Nicky Hunt and Javi Moreno for Per Frandsen, Jon Otsemobor and Djorkaeff.

But despite Okocha's best efforts, there was to be no dramatic comeback for Wanderers.

3 Manchester City

Kevin Davies keeps Richard Dunne at arms length.

Jussi Jaaskelainen clears upfield.

"I felt we had enough opportunities to win the game in the first 20 minutes, but we were guilty of poor finishing." — Sam Allardyce

Bolton Wanderers 1

Carling Cup Final
Sunday 29th February 2004
Venue: **Millennium Stadium**
Attendance: **72,634**
Referee: **M.A.Riley**

STARTING LINE-UPS

Jaaskelainen

Hunt   Thome   N'Gotty   Charlton

Frandsen   Campo   Okocha (c)

Nolan   Djorkaeff

Davies

Job

Juninho

Zenden   Doriva   Boateng   Mendieta

Queudrue   Southgate (c)   Ehiogu   Mills

Schwarzer

Poole, Barness,
Giannakopoulos
Moreno, Pedersen.

Jones, Riggott,
Downing, Ricketts
Maccarone.

"We rushed our play far too much, and really didn't threaten until the final minute or so." – Sam Allardyce

Bolton Wanderers suffered Carling Cup heartbreak after narrowly losing to Middlesbrough at the Millennium Stadium.

Boro made the perfect start, finding themselves two goals to the good after seven minutes.

Joseph-Desire Job gave the Teesiders the lead with barely two minutes on the clock.

Gaizka Mendieta made the most of some space on the right, eventually crossing to Bolo Zenden on the opposite flank. The flying Dutchman delivered an inch-perfect ball towards the far post to find Job, who had the easiest of chances to bundle the ball past Jussi Jaaskelainen.

Youri Djorkaeff went close to equalising on four minutes, but Mark Schwarzer managed to steer the Frenchman's shot away for a corner.

Emerson Thome then brought down Job in the area and referee Mike Riley rightly pointed to the spot. Zenden took the penalty, and although the on-loan Chelsea star slipped as he kicked the ball, it took a deflection off Jaaskelainen's foot to nestle into the net.

Wanderers fans had their hearts in their mouths on 17 minutes when Juninho's right-wing cross was sliced by Thome, fortunately it went out for a corner.

Wanderers managed to peg a goal back on 21 minutes with a massive slice of fortune.

Kevin Davies collected from Kevin Nolan and struck a fairly tame right-footer which somehow slipped through Schwarzer's grasp to put Wanderers back on track.

Wanderers then failed to capitalise on some good opportunities to level the score.

Just before the half-hour mark, Per Frandsen struck the post with Schwarzer well beaten. The ball rebounded to Djorkaeff, but the Frenchman was denied by a quick recovery save from the big keeper.

Three minutes later Djorkaeff found himself in space and lined up a volley, but the ball deflected off a Boro defender and went for a corner.

Djorkaeff had another chance less than a minute later, but his effort lacked power and precision.

Jay-Jay Okocha hit a low drive goalwards on the stroke of half time, but it was easily saved by Schwarzer.

Wanderers never really threatened the Boro goal for the final 45 minutes, despite the attack-minded introduction of substitutes Henrik Pedersen, Javi Moreno and Stelios.

Wanderers' one chance came on the hour mark when an unmarked Nolan collected Nicky Hunt's pinpoint cross, but he couldn't find a way past Schwarzer.

There were looks of utter desolation in the Wanderers players' faces as referee Riley blew for time and ended their Carling Cup dream.

2 Middlesbrough

Youri Djorkaeff has a shot at goal.

Kevin Davies tries to get past Franck Queudrue and Doriva.

Jussi Jaaskelainen fails to stop Zenden's spot-kick.

EVENT LINE

KICK OFF

2 ⚽ Job (Open Play)

7 ⚽ Zenden (Penalty)

21 ⚽ Davies (Open Play)

23 ▢ Frandsen (Foul)

23 ▢ Boateng (Ung Conduct)

39 ▢ Campo (Ung Conduct)

HALF TIME 1-2

63 ⇄ Frandsen (Off) Pedersen (On)

65 ⇄ Job (Off) Ricketts (On)

78 ⇄ Nolan (Off) Moreno (On)

87 ⇄ Hunt (Off) Stelios (On)

90 ▢ Ricketts (Ung Conduct)

FULL TIME 1-2

STATISTICS

8	Shots On Target	5
3	Shots Off Target	7
1	Hit Woodwork	0
4	Caught Offside	5
4	Corners	2
24	Fouls	16

Birmingham City 2

FIXTURE INFORMATION

Premiership
Saturday 6th March 2004
Venue: **St Andrews**
Attendance: **28,003**
Referee: **A.P.D'Urso**

PREMIERSHIP FIXTURE HISTORY

	Played:**2** Draws:**0**	Wins ⚽	⬜	⬛
Birmingham City	2	5	3	0
Bolton Wanderers	0	1	4	1

STARTING LINE-UPS

Maik Taylor

Tebily　Cunningham (c)　Mar Taylor　Upson

Johnson　Savage　Clemence　Hughes

Forssell　Morrison

Davies

Djorkaeff　　　Nolan

Okocha (c)　Campo　Frandsen

Barness　Charlton　N'Gotty　Hunt

Jaaskelainen

Cisse, John,
Kenna, Bennett,
Purse.

Pedersen, Ba,
Stelios, Poole,
Howey.

PREMIERSHIP MILESTONES

Per Frandsen made his 125th Premiership appearance.

Anthony Barness made his 75th appearance in the Premiership.

Wanderers' post-Carling Cup blues were compounded by a 2-0 defeat at the hands of Birmingham.

Sam Allardyce made two changes to the side that lost to Middlesbrough in the Carling Cup final, replacing Emerson Thome with Anthony Barness and moving Simon Charlton back alongside Bruno N'Gotty at the heart of the Wanderers defence, with Barness filling in at left-back.

Birmingham looked the more dangerous side from the off, with Mikael Forssell and Clinton Morrison pressing the Wanderers goal.

The first chance fell to City, as Morrison turned Charlton inside the Wanderers box and fired towards the far corner. Jussi Jaaskelainen made a fine save low to his right to prevent a certain goal for the Blues.

Oliver Tebilly fed Bryan Hughes on the edge of the Wanderers box after 22 minutes, but despite having plenty of time and space to place his shot, the midfielder managed to fire straight at Jaaskelainen.

Birmingham broke the deadlock a minute later, as Forssell collected from Morrison and drilled a left-footed shot into the bottom-right corner from the centre of the penalty area.

Henrik Pedersen replaced Youri Djorkaeff three minutes into the second half, as Wanderers tried to recover from their first-half display.

As the second period wore on, Kevin Nolan was pushed further upfield alongside Kevin Davies in the hope that a three-pronged attack of Pedersen, Davies and Nolan would pose a greater threat. It worked to a degree, but clear-cut chances remained few and far between, while Birmingham remained a constant threat on the counter.

Jay-Jay Okocha was replaced by Ibrahim Ba in the 64th minute, the Wanderers captain continuing a run of poor form since returning from the African Cup of Nations.

As he trudged down the tunnel, Okocha must have been wondering if he'd left his box of tricks in Tunisia.

It came as no surprise when Birmingham added a second in the 69th minute, Hughes nodding in a Damien Johnson cross at the far post.

The Whites nearly pulled one back in the 78th minute, as former Birmingham man Charlton pounced on a loose ball following a corner.

But Maik Taylor's double-save denied him his first score in a Wanderers shirt and his first league goal for six years.

0 Bolton Wanderers

EVENT LINE

24 ⚽ Forssell (Open Play)

HALF TIME 1-0

48 ⇄ **Djorkaeff (Off) Pedersen (On)**

63 ⇄ **Okocha (Off) Ba (On)**

69 ⚽ Hughes (Open Play)

76 ⇄ Clemence (Off) Cisse (On)

79 ⇄ **Frandsen (Off) Stelios (On)**

84 ▢ Savage (Ung Conduct)

86 ⇄ Forssell (Off) John (On)

86 ▢ **Hunt (Foul)**

88 ⇄ Johnson (Off) Kenna (On)

FULL TIME 2-0

Jay-Jay Okocha is held back by Stephen Clemence.

STATISTICS

This Season	This Match		This Season	This Match
111	6	Shots On Target	2	140
139	4	Shots Off Target	8	184
5	0	Hit Woodwork	0	9
56	2	Caught Offside	1	67
147	3	Corners	5	158
387	10	Fouls	15	364
45%	55%	Possession	45%	45%

PREMIERSHIP STANDINGS

Position (pos before)	W	D	L	F	A	Pts
5 (7) Birmingham	11	9	7	30	29	42
11 (11) Bolton	8	10	9	32	42	34

Kevin Nolan takes on Olivier Tebily.

"This is when you show your strength of character, because everyone can do the business when you're playing well."

— Simon Charlton

Bolton Wanderers 0

FIXTURE INFORMATION

Premiership
Saturday 13th March 2004
Venue: **Reebok Stadium**
Attendance: **26,717**
Referee: **G.Poll**

PREMIERSHIP FIXTURE HISTORY

Played:5 Draws:2	Wins ⚽	☐	■
Bolton Wanderers	2	6	6	0
Chelsea	1	6	7	1

STARTING LINE-UPS

Jaaskelainen

Hunt   Thome   N'Gotty   Charlton

Nolan   Campo   Okocha (c)

Stelios   Pedersen

Davies

Crespo   Hasselbaink

Duff   Lampard   Geremi   Gronkjaer

Bridge   Terry (c)   Desailly   Gallas

Ambrosio

Ba, Poole,   Cole, Huth,
Howey, Frandsen,   Parker, Melchiot,
Moreno.   Makabu-Makalambay.

PREMIERSHIP MILESTONES

Jussi Jaaskelainen made his 100th Premiership appearance.

100

Wanderers failed to make their superior first-half performance count as Chelsea staged a smash-and-grab raid at the Reebok Stadium to keep their Premiership title hopes alive.

The home side should have sailed to a comfortable victory after creating enough first-half chances to win two games.

But goals from John Terry and Damien Duff inside a three-minute spell with less than 20 minutes remaining ensured that Claudio Ranieri's men went away with all three points.

Marco Ambrosio – making his Premiership debut – was the busier of the two keepers, as Wanderers set about putting their recent disappointing performances behind them.

Kevin Nolan sent in a left-footed volley which went narrowly wide after six minutes.

Henrik Pedersen then hit the post after latching onto a Jussi Jaaskelainen free kick which had been flicked on by the heads of Kevin Davies and Stelios.

Next, Jay-Jay Okocha, who appeared to be back to his best, tested Ambrosio with a drive which the Italian did well to beat away.

The Nigerian followed that up with a rasping 20-yarder which the Italian keeper managed to turn away for a corner.

Okocha was thwarted again on 27 minutes when another long-range effort flew narrowly wide.

He then saw a free kick from the edge of the box go just over the bar, before Davies hit a 35-yard dipping volley which had Ambrosio scrambling to collect.

Okocha had another decent chance just after the restart, but his shot lacked the power of his previous efforts.

Frank Lampard registered the visitors' first meaningful effort on 51 minutes when he curled a superb effort from 25 yards. But Jaaskelainen read the shot well and turned the ball away for a corner.

Wanderers were no longer dominating as they had in the first period, and the Blues made them pay on 71 minutes when Jimmy Floyd Hasselbaink flicked on Duff's cross from the right, opening space for Terry to volley home from six yards.

The visitors doubled their lead three minutes later, as Jaaskelainen inadvertently helped Duff's tap-in into the back of the net.

Chelsea continued to press against a deflated Wanderers and were unlucky not to add to their goal tally.

As the game wound down, Okocha side-footed a good chance straight into the hands of Ambrosio to cap a frustrating afternoon for Wanderers.

2 Chelsea

Kevin Davies and Stelios challenge John Terry.

"We switched off for three minutes and got punished." – Stelios

Arsenal 2

FIXTURE INFORMATION

Premiership
Saturday 20th March 2004
Venue: **Highbury**
Attendance: **38,053**
Referee: **G.P.Barber**

PREMIERSHIP FIXTURE HISTORY

Played:5 Draws:1	Wins	●	▢	▪
Arsenal	4	11	6	0
Bolton Wanderers	0	5	6	2

STARTING LINE-UPS

Ljungberg, Cygan, Stack, Kanu, Reyes.

Frandsen, Poole, Barness, Vaz Te, Pezzarossi.

Treble-chasers Arsenal consigned Wanderers to their fourth consecutive league defeat.

The Gunners cruised to a 2-0 lead inside 25 minutes thanks to goals from Robert Pires and Dennis Bergkamp.

But a resurgent second-half display from Sam Allardyce's troops – buoyed by Ivan Campo's first goal of the season just before the break – helped to dispel their underdog status.

Kevin Nolan wasted a good chance on four minutes, scuffing his volley off Stelios's free kick from the right.

Thierry Henry went close a minute later, curling a 35-yarder against Jussi Jaaskelainen's bar.

The hosts were enjoying the majority of possession, and they made it count in the 16th minute, as Pires collected from Bergkamp and curled a shot past Jaaskelainen into the top corner.

Five minutes later, Jaaskelainen had to make a brave close-range save from Ashley Cole, as the pacey left-back latched onto a Pires pass from the right before stabbing the ball into the advancing Wanderers keeper.

But there was nothing the big Finn could do about Arsenal's second goal, which came on 24 minutes.

Pires's pass from the centre of the park found Henry out on the left. The Frenchman took advantage of a flat-footed Wanderers defence to square the ball to Bergkamp, whose exquisite finish nestled into the back of the net.

Wanderers pulled one back on 41 minutes, as Campo collected Stelios's in-swinging corner at the far post and fired past a bewildered Jens Lehmann

Wanderers were extremely unlucky not to go into the dressing room level when Stelios's header off Henrik Pedersen's left-wing cross clipped the bar.

Wanderers came out for the second period a much brighter side, and they should have equalised five minutes after the restart, but Kevin Davies somehow missed with his header.

Jaaskelainen had to be alert on the hour mark, clawing Henry's first-time shot out of the air with an acrobatic one-handed save.

Substitute Freddie Ljungberg – a 68th-minute replacement for Gilberto Silva – missed a prime opportunity to move the Gunners further ahead after 75 minutes.

Bergkamp broke the offside trap and promptly squared the ball to the Swede, who, under pressure from Simon Charlton, failed to connect with the ball.

Campo just failed to earn Wanderers a deserved point when he hooked a loose ball over Lehmann's bar in the final minute.

1 Bolton Wanderers

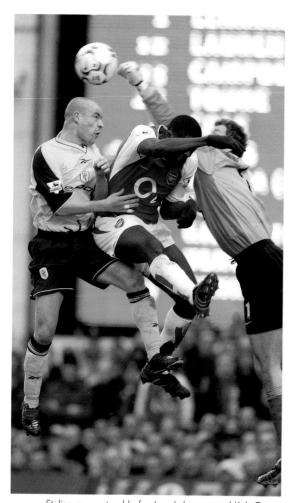

Stelios causes trouble for Jens Lehmann and Kolo Toure.

STATISTICS

This Season	This Match		This Season	This Match
181	7	Shots On Target	2	147
156	4	Shots Off Target	5	202
13	1	Hit Woodwork	1	11
90	2	Caught Offside	2	71
153	6	Corners	1	167
410	12	Fouls	18	392
54%	62%	Possession	38%	44%

PREMIERSHIP STANDINGS

Position (pos before)	W	D	L	F	A	Pts
1 (1) Arsenal	22	7	0	57	19	73
13 (13) Bolton	8	10	11	33	46	34

"We couldn't convert any of the chances we created in the second half, and I think that's quite worrying." — Simon Charlton

Bolton Wanderers 1

FIXTURE INFORMATION

Premiership

Sunday 28th March 2004

Venue: **Reebok Stadium**

Attendance: **27,360**

Referee: **M.L.Dean**

PREMIERSHIP FIXTURE HISTORY

Played:5 Draws:0	Wins	☺	▢	▆
Bolton Wanderers	3	7	7	1
Newcastle United	2	10	10	0

STARTING LINE-UPS

Jaaskelainen

Hunt Thome N'Gotty Charlton

Nolan Campo Okocha (c)

Stelios Pedersen

Davies

Shearer (c) Bellamy

Robert Speed Jenas Bowyer

Bernard Bramble Woodgate Taylor

Given

Howey, Frandsen, Poole, Vaz Te, Pezzarossi.

Viana, Ambrose, Ameobi, Harper, Elliott.

PREMIERSHIP MILESTONES

Bruno N'Gotty made his 75th appearance in the Premiership.

75

Henrik Pedersen's fourth goal of the season returned Wanderers to winning ways against Newcastle United.

The Dane struck in the fourth minute to put Wanderers in the driving seat for a game they fully deserved to win.

The home side were desperately unlucky not to double their advantage moments later when Titus Bramble handled the ball inside his own area. Wanderers' appeals for a penalty were waved away by referee Mike Dean.

Wanderers were playing with the same confidence they had shown against Arsenal and Chelsea in recent weeks, and were intent on attacking the Newcastle defence.

Jay-Jay Okocha let fly from distance, but the ball went just wide of Shay Given's goal.

Alan Shearer went for an overhead kick after good work from Craig Bellamy, but Jussi Jaaskelainen managed to clear the ball away.

Nicky Hunt then tested Given with a chipped effort, but his shot lacked the strength to trouble the Irish keeper.

The visitors wasted a glorious chance to get back in the game on 22 minutes when the pacey Bellamy took advantage of a mistake by Emerson Thome to gift himself a one-on-one opportunity with Jaaskelainen. But the Wanderers keeper and the backtracking Brazilian did enough to put off the former Norwich City striker, who fired hopelessly wide.

Jaaskelainen did well to steer away Jonathan Woodgate's powerful drive eight minutes later. There was some concern when the ball fell into the path of Bramble, but the defender drilled it high and wide.

Wanderers then regained their earlier momentum, Okocha testing Given with a powerful effort on 33 minutes.

Given did well to gather a long-range effort from Kevin Nolan five minutes before the break.

Steve Howey, who started the second half against his former team in place of the injured Bruno N'Gotty, couldn't prevent Shearer from charging towards goal and unleashing a shot, which fortunately flew narrowly wide.

Ivan Campo might have extended Wanderers' advantage on 55 minutes, but he lofted the ball over Given's bar.

Pedersen went on a strong run just after the hour mark, but was felled by Bramble before he could get into the box. Okocha failed to make the free kick count, firing straight into the defensive wall.

Wanderers did well to stifle the service to Bellamy and Shearer for the remainder of the game, and Jaaskelainen was hardly troubled as the home side clinched the win they so desperately craved.

0 Newcastle United

Simon Charlton blocks Laurent Robert.

Kevin Davies takes on Jonathan Woodgate.

EVENT LINE

4 ⊙ Pedersen (Open Play)

41 ☐ N'Gotty (Foul)

HALF TIME 1-0

46 ⇄ N'Gotty (Off) Howey (On)

63 ☐ Bramble (Foul)

71 ⇄ Hunt (Off) Frandsen (On)

72 ⇄ Bowyer (Off) Ambrose (On)

72 ⇄ Jenas (Off) Viana (On)

72 ⇄ Robert (Off) Ameobi (On)

83 ☐ Woodgate (Foul)

FULL TIME 1-0

STATISTICS

This Season	This Match		This Season	This Match
155	8	Shots On Target	4	141
211	9	Shots Off Target	8	168
11	0	Hit Woodwork	0	7
74	3	Caught Offside	1	98
174	7	Corners	6	199
403	11	Fouls	12	402
44%	42%	Possession	58%	49%

PREMIERSHIP STANDINGS

Position (pos before)	W	D	L	F	A	Pts
13 (14) **Bolton**	9	10	11	34	46	37
5 (5) Newcastle	11	12	7	41	31	45

"The second half was ours, and but for Shay Given we would have won comfortably."
— Sam Allardycece

# Middlesbrough 2

FIXTURE INFORMATION

Premiership
Saturday 3rd April 2004
Venue: **Riverside Stadium**
Attendance: **30,107**
Referee: **N.S.Barry**

PREMIERSHIP FIXTURE HISTORY

Played:4 Draws:1	Wins	⚽	⬜	⬛
Middlesbrough	2	6	7	0
Bolton Wanderers	1	5	10	0

STARTING LINE-UPS

Schwarzer

Mills   Ehiogu (c)   Riggott   Zenden

Mendieta   Boateng   Greening

Juninho

Maccarone   Job

Davies

Pedersen   Stelios

Okocha (c)   Campo   Nolan

Barness   Howey   Thome   Hunt

Jaaskelainen

Nemeth, Downing, Ricketts, Jones, Bates.

Frandsen, Moreno, Vaz Te, Poole, Charlton.

PREMIERSHIP MILESTONES

Ricardo Vaz Te made his Premiership debut.

An own-goal by Kevin Nolan and a Jonathan Greening strike carried Middlesbrough to a comfortable victory against their fellow Carling Cup finalists.

Wanderers, looking to avenge that disappointing Millennium Stadium defeat, almost opened the scoring in the first minute when Jay-Jay Okocha found Henrik Pedersen, but the forward hooked his effort wide.

The visitors then suffered an early blow, as Nolan freakishly put the ball past his own keeper after eight minutes.

Gaizka Mendieta's corner from the right was curling away from goal, but Nolan, in an attempt to clear the danger, guided the ball past Jussi Jaaskelainen to put Boro in front.

Wanderers responded almost immediately when Pedersen found himself charging on goal following good work from Anthony Barness and Kevin Davies. But the Dane's strike hit the foot of the post and was promptly cleared.

Boro pressed again in the 14th minute, as Juninho stole the ball in midfield and charged towards the Wanderers goal. But the Brazilian chose to ignore an unmarked Joseph-Desire Job at the far post and shot straight at the advancing Jaaskelainen, who managed to block the ball.

Boro should have doubled their lead just before the interval when an unmarked Juninho received the ball at the far post, but Jaaskelainen raced from his line to block the little midfielder's powerful strike.

Wanderers captain Okocha went close to equalising five minutes after the restart when he latched onto a short pass from Pedersen and fired at goal, only to see his effort fly narrowly wide.

But it was Boro who would score next, moving 2-0 ahead less than a minute later.

Mendieta got himself into a goalscoring position, but his effort was blocked. The ball rebounded into the path of an unmarked Greening, who took quick advantage of an easy knock-in.

Massimo Maccarone almost made it three when he ran down the left and curled in a splendid right-footed effort which was just inches away from the top corner.

With 12 minutes remaining, Okocha lined up a free kick just outside Boro's area. Although he managed to get the ball on target, keeper Mark Schwarzer dived the right way to make a comfortable save.

Jaaskelainen spared Wanderers' blushes right at the death when he made a brave save at the feet of former Wanderers star Michael Ricketts, who had earlier replaced Juninho.

A frustrating afternoon for Wanderers was summed up just before the whistle, as Okocha's free kick cannoned into the wall before being cleared.

0 Bolton Wanderers

Jay-Jay Okocha tries to go past Danny Mills

Ivan Campo directs a header towards goal.

STATISTICS

This Season	This Match		This Season	This Match
134	6	Shots On Target	3	158
165	7	Shots Off Target	8	219
4	1	Hit Woodwork	1	12
117	5	Caught Offside	2	76
143	7	Corners	8	182
467	16	Fouls	17	420
48%	58%	Possession	42%	44%

PREMIERSHIP STANDINGS

Position (pos before)	W	D	L	F	A	Pts
11 (11) Boro	11	8	12	37	39	41
13 (13) Bolton	9	10	12	34	48	37

"I'm bitterly disappointed with the performance and the result. Our goalkeeper was the only one who deserved any credit."
— Sam Allardyce

Bolton Wanderers 2

FIXTURE INFORMATION

Premiership
Saturday 10th April 2004
Venue: **Reebok Stadium**
Attendance: **26,374**
Referee: **M.D.Messias**

PREMIERSHIP FIXTURE HISTORY

Played:**5** Draws:**1**	Wins	☉	☐	■
Bolton Wanderers	2	6	9	1
Aston Villa	2	7	9	1

STARTING LINE-UPS

Jaaskelainen

Barness   Thome   N'Gotty   Charlton

Nolan Frandsen Okocha (c)

Djorkaeff   Pedersen

Davies

Crouch   Vassell

Barry Hitzlsperger McCann Hendrie

Samuel Ridgewell Mellberg (c) De la Cruz

Sorensen

Hunt, Campo, Stelios, Poole, Moreno.

L.Moore, Dublin, Whittingham, Postma, Johnsen.

PREMIERSHIP MILESTONES

Henrik Pedersen's goal was Bolton's 200th in the Premiership.

200

Kevin Davies timed his eighth goal of the season to perfection, as he helped Wanderers salvage a point which moved them to 12th in the table.

The Wanderers striker grabbed his first goal since the Carling Cup final to prevent his side from crashing to their sixth defeat in seven top-flight games.

Youri Djorkaeff, back after a hamstring injury, marked his recall with the game's opening chance after two minutes, as he latched onto Olof Mellberg's clearance and volleyed just wide.

The Frenchman turned provider six minutes later, whipping in a corner which compatriot Bruno N'Gotty headed wide.

He then hit a low drive in the 13th minute which was just off target.

Villa got in on the act three minutes later when Gareth Barry placed a left-footer just wide of Jussi Jaaskelainen's goal.

And the visitors took the lead two minutes later, through 6ft 6in striker Peter Crouch.

Barry swung in a great left-wing cross which the former Portsmouth and QPR striker managed to nod past Jaaskelainen, despite the attention of Simon Charlton.

Wanderers countered with a Per Frandsen lob which failed to trouble Thomas Sorensen.

Wanderers captain Jay-Jay Okocha, still without a Premiership goal, stung the Danish keeper's fingertips on the half-hour mark with a rasping drive. Davies then hit a shot on the turn over the bar.

Sorensen had to be at his sharpest to deny countryman Frandsen on 37 minutes, after the Wanderers midfielder had collected Djorkaeff's short free kick.

The home side didn't have to wait long to get back in the game, as Henrik Pedersen hit his second successive league goal at the Reebok Stadium just three minutes after the restart.

A clearance from Ulises De La Cruz rebounded off Okocha into the path of Pedersen, who was decisive from close range.

But Villa restored their advantage just four minutes later, as Lee Hendrie latched onto a long pass from Barry and hit a great lob over Jaaskelainen.

Darius Vassell almost extended his side's lead on 55 minutes when he collected another long ball from Barry, but Jaaskelainen did well to prevent the England man from scoring.

The hard-working Djorkaeff planted a header wide on 81 minutes before being replaced by Stelios.

And then came Wanderers' dramatic late equaliser, as Stelios crossed for Davies to fire home in the 86th minute.

2 Aston Villa

Henrik Pedersen levels for Bolton just after half time.

Jay-Jay Okocha is bundled over by Thomas Hitzlsperger.

"Jussi's kept us in the game again."
— Kevin Davies

EVENT LINE

18 ⚽ Crouch (Open Play)

HALF TIME 0-1

46 ⇄ **Charlton (Off) Hunt (On)**

48 ⚽ **Pedersen (Open Play)**

53 ⚽ Hendrie (Open Play)

62 ▢ Crouch (Foul)

62 ▢ Hendrie (Ung Conduct)

65 ⇄ Vassell (Off) Moore L (On)

68 ⇄ Crouch (Off) Dublin (On)

71 ▢ Moore L (Dissent)

79 ⇄ **Nolan (Off) Campo (On)**

79 ⇄ Hendrie (Off) Whittingham (On)

81 ⇄ **Djorkaeff (Off) Stelios (On)**

86 ⚽ **Davies (Open Play)**

89 ▢ **Campo (Ung Conduct)**

FULL TIME 2-2

STATISTICS

This Season	This Match		This Season	This Match
165	7	Shots On Target	3	151
228	9	Shots Off Target	4	198
12	0	Hit Woodwork	0	10
78	2	Caught Offside	3	129
188	6	Corners	4	207
430	10	Fouls	12	497
44%	45%	Possession	55%	46%

PREMIERSHIP STANDINGS

Position (pos before)	W	D	L	F	A	Pts
12 (14) **Bolton**	9	11	12	36	50	38
7 (7) Aston Villa	12	9	11	41	38	45

Wolves 1

FIXTURE INFORMATION

Premiership

Monday 12th April 2004

Venue: **Molineux**

Attendance: **28,695**

Referee: **U.D.Rennie**

PREMIERSHIP FIXTURE HISTORY

Played:1 Draws:0	Wins	⚽	◻	◼
Wolves	0	1	2	0
Bolton Wanderers	1	2	1	0

STARTING LINE-UPS

Jones

Irwin Okoronkwo Butler Naylor

Newton Ince (c) Cameron Kennedy

Camara Cort

Davies

Pedersen Stelios

Frandsen Campo (c) Nolan

Barness N'Gotty Thome Hunt

Jaaskelainen

Miller, Oakes, Craddock, Ganea, Gudjonsson.

Okocha, Djorkaeff, Poole, Charlton, Moreno.

PREMIERSHIP MILESTONES

Kevin Nolan made his 100th Premiership appearance.

100

Kevin Davies' second goal in two games – and ninth of the season – earned Wanderers an injury-time victory against battling Wolves.

Wolves were in attacking mood as the game got underway, Mark Kennedy making a strong run down the left flank before crashing to the ground inside the Wanderers box. The Molineux faithful looked for a penalty, but referee Uriah Rennie correctly waved the game on.

Wanderers had a chance six minutes later when Ivan Campo headed over a right-wing cross from Stelios.

Per Frandsen might have broken the deadlock on 19 minutes when Stelios and Kevin Nolan combined to set him up, but the Danish midfielder shot wide while under pressure from the Wolves defence.

Former England captain Paul Ince almost put the hosts in front when his header off a Kennedy corner went just the wrong side of Jussi Jaaskelainen's right-hand post.

Jaaskelainen made a great diving save to turn Colin Cameron's drive away for a corner on 33 minutes.

The game then exploded into life with two goals in two minutes.

First, Henrik Pedersen headed home off Campo's cross for his third goal in four games.

Then, moments later, Henri Camara equalised with a spectacular curling effort.

Davies almost restored Wanderers' lead deep into first-half injury time, but Paul Jones made a great save to turn his shot away.

Campo wasted a good opportunity to put Wanderers back in front when he scooped the ball over Jones's bar from close range after the Wolves defence had failed to clear a corner.

Chances were few and far between for both sides in the second half, and neither keeper was seriously tested.

Davies headed over for Wanderers, while Carl Cort scuffed his volley wide for Wolves.

Jay-Jay Okocha, still searching for his first league goal of the season, then fired a free kick high and wide. He followed up with a poke off a Jones spill which went inches wide.

Camara's cross then almost found its way past Jaaskelainen, as Nolan's attempted clearance sliced away for a corner.

Wanderers had Nicky Hunt to thank for keeping the scores level when he cleared Ince's header off the line with just two minutes to go.

And it was Wanderers who had the last laugh, thanks to the in-form Davies.

2 Bolton Wanderers

Henrik Pedersen is congratulated after giving Bolton the lead.

STATISTICS

This Season	This Match		This Season	This Match
134	6	Shots On Target	5	170
210	7	Shots Off Target	14	242
10	0	Hit Woodwork	0	12
69	1	Caught Offside	7	85
156	6	Corners	9	197
467	13	Fouls	11	441
45%	51%	Possession	49%	44%

PREMIERSHIP STANDINGS

Position (pos before)	W	D	L	F	A	Pts
20 (20) Wolves	5	10	18	31	71	25
12 (12) Bolton	10	11	12	38	51	41

Emerson Thome tackles Henri Camara.

"For all intents and purposes, those three points will secure us in the Premiership."
— Sam Allardyce

Bolton Wanderers 2

FIXTURE INFORMATION

Premiership
Saturday 17th April 2004
Venue: **Reebok Stadium**
Attendance: **26,440**
Referee: **J.T.Winter**

PREMIERSHIP FIXTURE HISTORY

Played:**5** Draws:**2**	Wins	☺	☐	◼
Bolton Wanderers	2	7	4	0
Tottenham Hotspur	1	5	11	0

STARTING LINE-UPS

Barness, Frandsen, Stelios, Poole, Moreno.

Taricco, Keane, Ricketts, Hirschfeld, Bunjevcevic.

Wanderers equalled their best-ever Premiership points tally with a 2-0 victory over Tottenham.

Goals in each half from Ivan Campo and Henrik Pedersen lifted Wanderers to last season's total of 44 points.

Sam Allardyce recalled Youri Djorkaeff and Jay-Jay Okocha to the starting line-up, after the pair were on the substitutes bench for the game at Wolves.

Simon Charlton was also in the starting 11, at the expense of Anthony Barness.

Wanderers gave an early glimpse of the dominance they would enjoy throughout the match when Charlton lofted a ball upfield in the second minute. Pedersen slipped away from his marker and controlled the ball in the Spurs box, but he could only manage to fire across the face of Kasey Keller's goal.

The home side made the breakthrough five minutes later, courtesy of Campo's fourth goal of the campaign.

The former Real Madrid ace received a pass from Okocha and fired a shot from 25 yards. The ball bounced over Keller and into the back of the net.

The American keeper did a much better job when he dived to deny Kevin Nolan's lob.

Jermain Defoe might have done better when he pounced on a mistake by Emerson Thome, only to fire wide.

Okocha cut in from the right a minute after the restart, but he fired his shot over Keller's bar.

Spurs finally registered their first effort on target in the 51st minute when Michael Brown hit a low drive straight at Jaaskelainen, who was celebrating his 200th league start for Wanderers.

Okocha fired in a vicious free kick two minutes later, only to see Keller turn the ball away for a corner.

The industrious Kevin Davies might have extended Wanderers' lead on 62 minutes, but he dragged his effort across goal.

Pedersen then took advantage of an Anthony Gardner slip to net his fourth goal in five games and dispel any fears of a Spurs comeback.

Gardner out-paced the in-form Dane as the two raced for Djorkaeff's through-ball. But the defender's momentum caused him to lose possession, allowing Pedersen to place a right-footer past Keller.

Wanderers' lead was never in doubt, as Spurs appeared every inch the out-of-form team they were.

While Wanderers could now look forward to a fourth consecutive season in the Premiership, the North London outfit's top-flight future remained uncertain.

0 Tottenham Hotspur

Emerson Thome clears, with Fredi Kanoute lurking.

Kevin Davies gets ahead of Anthony Gardner.

"You need a man in form to capitalise on a mistake, and we had that man in Henrik Pedersen." — Sam Allardyce

EVENT LINE

7 ⚽ Campo (Open Play)

HALF TIME 1-0

46 🔄 Poyet (Off) Taricco (On)

61 🔄 Redknapp (Off) Keane (On)

65 ⚽ Pedersen (Open Play)

70 ▢ Campo (Foul)

76 🔄 Hunt (Off) Barness (On)

80 ▢ Davies (Foul)

82 🔄 Davies (Off) Ricketts (On)

86 🔄 Okocha (Off) Frandsen (On)

87 🔄 Djorkaeff (Off) Stelios (On)

90 ▢ Taricco (Foul)

FULL TIME 2-0

STATISTICS

This Season	This Match		This Season	This Match
175	5	Shots On Target	2	163
251	9	Shots Off Target	5	199
12	0	Hit Woodwork	0	5
87	2	Caught Offside	2	96
208	11	Corners	4	175
460	19	Fouls	23	540
44%	45%	Possession	55%	47%

PREMIERSHIP STANDINGS

Position (pos before)	W	D	L	F	A	Pts
12 (12) Bolton	11	11	12	40	51	44
14 (14) Tottenham	11	5	18	42	54	38

Southampton 1

FIXTURE INFORMATION

Premiership

Saturday 24th April 2004

Venue: **Friends Provident St Mary's Stadium**

Attendance: **31,712**

Referee: **S.W.Dunn**

PREMIERSHIP FIXTURE HISTORY

	Played: **5** Draws: **2**	Wins	⚽	▢	▨
Southampton		1	2	9	1
Bolton Wanderers		2	3	12	0

STARTING LINE-UPS

Niemi

Telfer Lundekvam Higginbotham Le Saux

Prutton Folly Delap Pahars

Phillips Beattie (c)

Davies

Pedersen Djorkaeff

Okocha (c) Campo Nolan

Charlton N'Gotty Thome Barness

Jaaskelainen

Hall, A.Svensson,
Fernandes, Smith,
Ormerod.

Hunt, Frandsen,
Stelios, Ricketts,
Moreno.

Kevin Davies returned to haunt his old club as he fired the winner against Southampton to make it three wins on the trot for Wanderers.

The big striker hit his 10th goal of the season less than two minutes after Kevin Nolan had fired an equaliser following Marian Pahars' first-half opener.

Wanderers almost seized a 5th-minute lead when skipper Jay-Jay Okocha clipped Antti Niemi's bar with a 30-yard drive. It was his 100th shot of the season.

Saints suffered an early blow after nine minutes when Graeme Le Saux limped off with a hamstring injury. Fitz Hall replaced the former Chelsea man.

Kevin Phillips, scorer of 10 goals in 12 games, registered Saints' first serious effort when his overhead kick went wide of Jussi Jaaskelainen's right-hand post.

A minute later, strike partner James Beattie headed Paul Telfer's corner over the bar after shaking off the attention of Bruno N'Gotty.

Pahars then opened the scoring for Saints, lobbing Jaaskelainen after collecting a great diagonal ball from Telfer.

It took a stunning block from Niemi to deny the visitors an equaliser on 26 minutes.

Wanderers worked their way into the Saints box and eventually Nolan released Davies on the far side. The former Southampton hitman raced towards goal and fired in a shot, but the Finnish keeper was on hand to make the save.

Davies enjoyed another good opportunity less than a minute after the restart, as some neat football involving Youri Djorkaeff and Henrik Pedersen opened space for the Wanderers striker to power a drive from distance which unfortunately went over the bar.

Sam Allardyce replaced Pedersen with compatriot Per Frandsen on 50 minutes.

Wanderers began to dominate the game during the opening stages of the second half, as they passed well and enjoyed plenty of possession.

Their persistence paid off in the space of two scintillating minutes, when they not only equalised but managed to sneak the lead.

First, Davies' cross to the far post found Nolan, who placed his header past the despairing dive of Niemi to claim his 11th goal of the season.

Then, a minute later, Okocha found the head of Davies with a brilliant right-wing cross, which he planted past Niemi to leapfrog Wanderers ahead of Southampton and into 10th position.

2 Bolton Wanderers

Kevin Davies the win with Kevin Nolan and Ivan Campo.

Kevin Nolan heads Wanderers level.

"Kevin was in the right spot and just had to let it hit his head, and the pace took it past the keeper." — Sam Allardyce

EVENT LINE

10 ⚽ Le Saux (Off) Hall (On)

21 ⦿ Pahars (Open Play)

23 ☐ Phillips (Ung Conduct)

26 ☐ Nolan (Foul)

39 ☐ Campo (Ung Conduct)

43 ☐ Telfer (Foul)

HALF TIME 1-0

46 ⚽ Barness (Off) Hunt (On)

48 ⚽ Delap (Off) Svensson A (On)

50 ⚽ Pedersen (Off) Frandsen (On)

60 ☐ Folly (Foul)

62 ☐ Thome (Foul)

77 ⚽ Djorkaeff (Off) Stelios (On)

77 ⦿ Nolan (Open Play)

78 ⦿ Davies (Open Play)

79 ⚽ Pahars (Off) Fernandes (On)

90 ☐ Svensson A (Foul)

FULL TIME 1-2

STATISTICS

This Season	This Match		This Season	This Match
157	3	Shots On Target	7	182
187	6	Shots Off Target	4	255
9	0	Hit Woodwork	1	13
106	2	Caught Offside	4	91
203	2	Corners	2	210
454	14	Fouls	16	476
46%	43%	Possession	57%	45%

PREMIERSHIP STANDINGS

Position (pos before)	W	D	L	F	A	Pts
11 (9) Southampton	12	9	13	39	35	45
10 (12) Bolton	12	11	12	42	52	47

Bolton Wanderers 4

FIXTURE INFORMATION

Premiership
Sunday 2nd May 2004
Venue: **Reebok Stadium**
Attendance: **27,420**
Referee: **S.G.Bennett**

PREMIERSHIP FIXTURE HISTORY

	Wins	☺	▢	■
Played:**5** Draws:**0**				
Bolton Wanderers	1	6	11	0
Leeds United	4	12	12	1

STARTING LINE-UPS

Jaaskelainen

Hunt Thome N'Gotty Charlton

Nolan Campo Okocha (c)

Djorkaeff Davies Pedersen

Viduka Smith

Milner Matteo (c) McPhail Pennant

Harte Caldwell Duberry Kelly

Robinson

Barness, Moreno,
Stelios, Poole,
Frandsen.

Wilcox, Carson,
Kilgallon, Lennon,
Barmby.

A fantastic second-half recovery saw Wanderers fight back from a goal behind to clinch an emphatic victory against 10-man Leeds United.

Two goals from Youri Djorkaeff, an Ian Harte own-goal and Kevin Nolan's 12th strike of the season earned Wanderers their fourth successive victory.

The spectre of relegation haunted Eddie Gray's men from the off, and they could have fallen behind as early as the fourth minute when Henrik Pedersen's shot deflected off Stephen McPhail for a corner.

Two minutes later, the Dane charged down the left flank and knocked in a good cross for Djorkaeff, whose shot cannoned off a Leeds defender for another Wanderers corner.

Paul Robinson came to Leeds' rescue on 16 minutes when he turned Kevin Davies' shot away for a corner.

Much against the run of play, Leeds found themselves a goal in front on 27 minutes when referee Steve Bennett awarded the Yorkshiremen a penalty for Emerson Thome's challenge on Alan Smith.

The Wanderers players were infuriated by the official's decision and Pedersen was later booked for his protests.

Mark Viduka stepped up to take the penalty and fired a powerful shot past the despairing dive of Jussi Jaaskelainen.

Viduka earned a yellow card four minutes later for lashing out at Thome. He was dismissed 90 seconds after that for a second bookable offence, an elbow to Bruno N'Gotty.

Djorkaeff cancelled the visitors' advantage just two minutes after the restart, as he controlled Jay-Jay Okocha's great pass and delicately placed the ball past Robinson.

Davies almost put Wanderers ahead two minutes later, but he flashed his shot wide.

Gary Kelly then kept things level with a superb headed clearance off his own line after Djorkaeff's powerful strike had beaten Robinson.

But two minutes later Djorkaeff put his side in front, firing home after Robinson could only parry Nicky Hunt's left-footed shot.

Wanderers increased their lead two minutes later, when Harte converted Pedersen's left-wing cross past his own keeper.

Robinson made another fantastic save to deny Djorkaeff on 56 minutes, but the Leeds keeper couldn't do anything about Wanderers' fourth goal, as Okocha played a superb through-ball into the box, allowing Nolan to place a deft left-footer past the advancing Robinson.

Wanderers now stood in 7th place on 50 points. With two games to go, an even higher return beckoned.

1 Leeds United

Kevin Nolan and Kevin Davies celebrate Bolton's fourth goal.

Youri Djorkaeff celebrates one of his two goals.

"The quality of our foreign players shone through in the second half. It was a pleasure to watch them play." — Sam Allardyce

EVENT LINE

27 ☐ Thome (Foul)

27 ⚽ Viduka (Penalty)

31 ☐ Viduka (Foul)

33 ▮ Viduka (Foul)

34 ☐ Hunt (Dissent)

38 ⇄ Thome (Off) Barness (On)

HALF TIME 0-1

47 ⚽ Djorkaeff (Open Play)

53 ⚽ Djorkaeff (Open Play)

55 ⚽ Harte (Own Goal)

56 ☐ Pennant (Foul)

58 ☐ Davies (Foul)

60 ⇄ Milner (Off) Wilcox (On)

69 ⇄ Pedersen (Off) Moreno (On)

78 ⚽ Nolan (Open Play)

84 ⇄ Davies (Off) Stelios (On)

FULL TIME 4-1

STATISTICS

This Season	This Match		This Season	This Match
192	10	Shots On Target	3	134
263	8	Shots Off Target	3	173
13	0	Hit Woodwork	0	8
96	5	Caught Offside	4	114
219	9	Corners	3	192
490	14	Fouls	21	547
45%	63%	Possession	37%	44%

PREMIERSHIP STANDINGS

Position (pos before)	W	D	L	F	A	Pts
7 (10) **Bolton**	13	11	12	46	53	50
19 (18) Leeds	8	8	20	37	75	32

Everton 1

FIXTURE INFORMATION

Premiership
Saturday 8th May 2004
Venue: **Goodison Park**
Attendance: **40,190**
Referee: **P.A.Durkin**

PREMIERSHIP FIXTURE HISTORY

	Played: 5	Draws: 1	Wins ☉	☐	◼
Everton	3	10	5		1
Bolton Wanderers	1	5	8		1

STARTING LINE-UPS

Martyn

Hibbert Yobo Weir (c) Pistone

Watson Osman Nyarko McFadden

Rooney Ferguson

Pedersen Davies Djorkaeff

Okocha (c) Campo Nolan

Charlton N'Gotty Thome Hunt

Jaaskelainen

Carsley, Radzinski,
Campbell, Wright,
Linderoth.

Frandsen, Barness,
Gardner, Poole,
Stelios.

Youri Djorkaeff bagged his second brace inside a week to help Wanderers make it five wins on the trot, their best run in the top flight since 1927.

The Frenchman struck a late winner after Duncan Ferguson had cancelled out his first-half opener, increasing Wanderers' points tally to a remarkable 53 in the process.

Everton started the brighter of the sides and could have taken the lead on two occasions in the opening four minutes.

First, Emerson Thome had to be at his most alert on two minutes, clearing Leon Osman's cross over his own bar with a number of Everton players lurking.

Then, on four minutes, Toffees skipper Ferguson fired over from 25 yards.

Henrik Pedersen registered Wanderers' first effort less than a minute later, heading wide off Jay-Jay Okocha's cross.

Nicky Hunt then came to Wanderers' rescue when he cleared Ferguson's scuffed effort from under his own bar.

From then on the visitors took control of the game, with the hosts allowing them plenty of space and time on the ball.

Kevin Davies picked out Pedersen with a delightful through-ball, but the Danish striker shot wide.

Kevin Nolan hit an effort just over the bar five minutes later, after receiving Okocha's long throw-in from the right.

Wanderers' pressure paid off on 14 minutes when Djorkaeff collected from Nolan, twisted and turned past his marker, and placed the ball past the advancing Nigel Martyn.

Everton boss David Moyes made two attack-minded substitutions during the interval, with Tomasz Radzinski and Lee Carsley coming on for Alessandro Pistone and Alex Nyarko.

The impact was almost immediate, as both players went close to an equaliser within five minutes of the restart.

First, Carsley glanced a header narrowly wide. Then, less than a minute later, Jussi Jaaskelainen managed to beat away Radzinski's close-range volley at the far post.

Wanderers responded by going close to extending their lead twice in quick succession.

Nolan tried to chip Martyn from 18 yards, only to see his effort fly narrowly off target. Pedersen then flashed a great cross across the face of goal, with Davies only inches from connecting.

The hosts restored parity on 68 minutes, as Ferguson fired home Radzinski's cross from the right.

Djorkaeff's dramatic late score then won it for Wanderers, his side-footed shot taking a deflection off Steve Watson before settling into the back of the net.

2 Bolton Wanderers

Simon Charlton congratulates goalscorer Youri Djorkaeff.

STATISTICS

This Season	This Match		This Season	This Match
173	4	Shots On Target	2	194
224	8	Shots Off Target	11	274
12	1	Hit Woodwork	0	13
96	5	Caught Offside	3	99
239	7	Corners	3	222
463	15	Fouls	11	501
47%	56%	Possession	44%	45%

PREMIERSHIP STANDINGS

Position (pos before)	W	D	L	F	A	Pts
16 (15) Everton	9	12	16	44	52	39
7 (7) Bolton	14	11	12	48	54	53

Emerson Thome challenges James McFadden.

"Youri was top drawer all game." "
— Sam Allardyce

Bolton Wanderers 0

FIXTURE INFORMATION

Premiership
Saturday 15th May 2004
Venue: **Reebok Stadium**
Attendance: **27,383**
Referee: **G.P.Barber**

PREMIERSHIP FIXTURE HISTORY

	Played:3	Draws:2	Wins ⚽	⬜	⬛
Bolton Wanderers	0	0	3	0
Fulham	1	2	4	0

STARTING LINE-UPS

Jaaskelainen

Hunt　Thome　N'Gotty　Charlton

Frandsen　Campo　Okocha (c)

Nolan　　　　　　Djorkaeff

Davies

McBride

Boa Morte　　　　　Malbranque

Legwinski (c)　Djetou　S.Davis

Bocanegra　Goma　Pearce　Volz

van der Sar

Gardner, Pedersen, Stelios, Ricketts, Barness.

John, Crossley, Hudson, Inamoto, Petta.

Two breakaway goals from Brian McBride gave Fulham a season-ending victory over Wanderers.

Per Frandsen, the club's current longest serving player, was made captain for the day. With his future still undecided, the Danish midfielder was given a rousing reception by the Wanderers faithful when he was replaced in the 71st minute by Stelios.

Fulham received an early scare when Jay-Jay Okocha launched a long throw into the box in the opening minute. The Cottagers failed to clear the ball, allowing Nicky Hunt to go close with a strike.

Frandsen then tried a snapshot in the 11th minute which keeper Edwin van der Sar handled comfortably.

Fulham displayed their attacking threat just moments later, as Sean Davis fired wide after collecting Luis Boa Morte's long throw-in.

Kevin Davies missed the first of a hat-trick of chances a minute later. The burly striker did all the hard work when he dispossessed Alain Goma just outside the Fulham area. As Goma lay prostrate, Davies charged towards goal with only Van der Sar to beat, but the giant Dutchman's frame blocked his effort.

Okocha then went close after good work from Youri Djorakeff and Frandsen.

The Nigerian midfielder, unbelievably still searching for his first Premiership goal of the campaign, almost found that elusive score when Ivan Campo was felled just outside the Fulham box on 22 minutes. Okocha fired in a free kick which had Van der Sar well beaten, but the ball struck the bar and rebounded to safety.

Fulham opened the scoring just before the half time whistle, as Carlos Bocanegra's cross to the far post found an unmarked McBride, who simply headed past Jussi Jaaskelainen.

Ricardo Gardner replaced Simon Charlton during the interval as Sam Allardyce looked to get Wanderers back in the game.

Davies spurned another opportunity on the hour mark when he connected with substitute Henrik Pedersen's left-wing cross, only to see Van der Sar make a close-range save to deny the Wanderers striker a deserved equaliser.

Then, with Wanderers chasing hard, McBride added his second to put the game beyond reach.

Davies missed his third chance when he fired another great cross from Pedersen just the wrong side of the Fulham goal.

The loss might have allowed Charlton Athletic to leapfrog Wanderers into 7th place, but Allardyce and his men still left the field to a rousing chorus of cheers.

"The crowd has been fantastic all season. "
— Sam Allardyce

2 Fulham

Stelios gets away from Sean Davis.

EVENT LINE

45 ⚽ McBride (Open Play)

HALF TIME 0-1

46 ⇄ Charlton (Off) Gardner (On)

59 ⇄ Djorkaeff (Off) Pedersen (On)

60 ▢ Davies (Foul)

71 ⇄ Frandsen (Off) Stelios (On)

78 ⚽ McBride (Open Play)

86 ▢ Boa Morte (Ung Conduct)

90 ⇄ McBride (Off) John (On)

FULL TIME 0-2

STATISTICS

This Season	This Match		This Season	This Match
199	5	Shots On Target	4	181
286	12	Shots Off Target	2	208
14	1	Hit Woodwork	0	9
103	4	Caught Offside	2	88
232	10	Corners	3	157
513	12	Fouls	18	578
45%	54%	Possession	46%	47%

PREMIERSHIP STANDINGS

Position (pos before)		W	D	L	F	A	Pts
8 (7)	Bolton	14	11	13	48	56	53
9 (9)	Fulham	14	10	14	52	46	52

End of Season Review

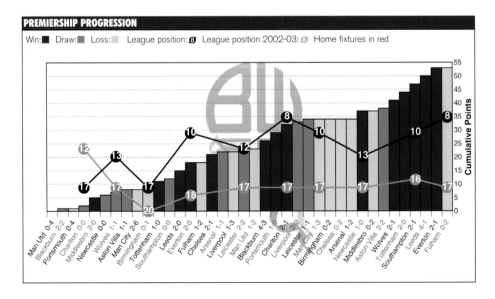

Reserves

Date	Opposition	Venue	Scoreline
11 Aug 03	Everton	H	L 1-4
1 Sep 03	Middlesbrough	H	L 0-2
9 Sep 03	Manchester City	A	L 0-2
15 Sep 03	Aston Villa	H	L 1-3
29 Sep 03	Newcastle United	H	L 2-3
8 Oct 03	Birmingham City	A	L 1-2
15 Oct 03	Sunderland	H	W 2-1
22 Oct 03	West Bromwich Albion	A	L 1-3
29 Oct 03	Leeds United	H	L 1-3
5 Nov 03	Blackburn Rovers	A	D 1-1
10 Nov 03	Manchester United	H	L 1-2
17 Nov 03	Manchester City	A	L 0-2
8 Dec 03	Aston Villa	A	L 0-2
17 Dec 03	Liverpool	A	L 1-3
18 Feb 04	Sunderland	A	L 0-1
23 Feb 04	West Bromwich Albion	H	D 1-1
2 March 04	Birmingham City	H	W 2-0
4 March 04	Leeds United	A	L 0-1
8 March 04	Newcastle United	A	W 3-2
16 March 04	Wolverhampton W.	A	L 2-4
22 March 04	Blackburn Rovers	H	L 0-3
31 March 04	Wolverhampton W.	H	L 2-4
8 April 04	Manchester United	A	L 0-2
14 April 04	Everton	A	L 0-1
20 April 04	Middlesbrough	A	D 0-0
26 April 04	Liverpool	H	D 2-2

Pos	Team	Pl	W	D	L	F	A	Diff	Pts
1	Aston Villa	26	17	5	4	55	31	24	56
2	Liverpool	26	14	8	4	41	21	20	50
3	Man Utd	26	13	8	5	55	39	16	47
4	Newcastle	26	13	4	9	50	42	8	43
5	Man City	26	11	8	7	34	24	10	41
6	Blackburn	26	11	6	9	49	45	4	39
7	Everton	26	10	8	8	37	33	4	38
8	Leeds	26	10	7	9	40	40	0	37
9	Mid'brough	26	8	10	8	33	33	0	34
10	Sunderland	26	8	7	11	37	46	-9	31
11	West Brom	26	8	6	12	36	48	-12	30
12	Birmingham	26	6	5	15	28	42	-14	23
13	W'hampton	26	4	6	16	27	49	-22	18
14	**Bolton**	**26**	**3**	**4**	**19**	**22**	**51**	**-29**	**13**

Academy Under 19

Date	Opposition	Venue	Scoreline
23 Aug 03	Chelsea	H	W 4-1
30 Aug 03	Ipswich Town	A	L 2-3
6 Sep 03	Derby County	H	W 7-2
27 Sep 03	Sheffield United	A	W 3-0
4 Oct 03	Stoke City	A	L 2-4
11 Oct 03	Crewe Alexandra	H	L 1-3
18 Oct 03	Wolverhampton W.	A	D 1-1
25 Oct 03	Everton	H	L 0-2
1 Nov 03	Manchester City	A	L 0-1
8 Nov 03	Liverpool	A	D 2-2
15 Nov 03	Blackburn Rovers	H	L 0-4
22 Nov 03	Manchester United	A	W 3-0
13 Dec 03	Everton	A	W 2-1
10 Jan 04	Manchester City	H	L 2-3
17 Jan 04	Liverpool	H	L 0-3
24 Jan 04	Blackburn Rovers	A	D 1-1
7 Feb 04	Manchester United	H	L 1-3
11 Feb 04	Sunderland	H	L 1-2
14 Feb 04	Sheffield Wednesday	A	D 2-2
21 Feb 04	Stoke City	H	W 3-1
28 Feb 04	Crewe Alexandra	A	W 2-0
6 Mar 04	Wolverhampton W.	H	L 1-2
13 Mar 04	Sheffield Wednesday	H	L 0-2
20 Mar 04	Leeds United	A	L 1-2
27 Mar 04	Newcastle United	A	W 3-1
3 April 04	Middlesbrough	H	W 1-0

Pos	Team	Pl	W	D	L	F	A	Diff	Pts
1	Man. City	26	20	2	4	58	24	34	62
2	Blackburn R.	26	13	7	6	42	25	17	46
3	Liverpool	26	12	9	5	46	36	10	45
4	Crewe Alex.	26	10	9	7	40	36	4	39
5	Everton	26	10	8	8	36	37	-1	38
6	Man. United	26	10	7	9	38	36	2	37
7	Wolves	26	9	8	9	38	32	6	35
8	**Bolton**	**26**	**8**	**4**	**14**	**39**	**52**	**-13**	**28**
9	Stoke City	26	4	7	15	37	63	-26	19
10	Sheff. Wed.	26	4	6	16	31	50	-19	18

All-Time Records

Club Facts and Records

Name:
Bolton Wanderers Football Club
Year Formed: **1874**
Turned Professional: **1880**
Ltd Co: **1895**
Previous Name:
1874 Christ Church FC;
1877 Bolton Wanderers
Club Nickname:
Trotters, Superwhites
Previous Grounds:
Park Recreation Ground, Cockle's Field,
Pike's Lane 1881; Burnden Park 1895;
Reebok Stadium 1997
First Football League Game:
8th September 1888, v Derby County (h) L 3-6
Most League Points:
61 (two for a win) FL3 1972-73,
98 (three for a win) FL1, 1996-97
Highest League Scorer in a season:
Joe Smith, 38, FL1, 1920-21
Most League goals In total:
Nat Lofthouse, 255, 1946-61
Most League goals In one match:
5, Tony Caldwell v Walsall, FL3, 10-09-1983
Most capped player:
Mark Fish, 34, South Africa
Most League Appearances:
Eddie Hopkinson, 519, 1956-70
Youngest League Player:
Ray Parry,15 years 267 days v
Wolverhampton Wanderers, 13-10-1951
Record Transfer Fee received:
£4,500,000 from Liverpool for Jason Mcateer,
September 1995
Record Transfer Fee Paid:
£3,500,000 for Dean Holdsworth from
Wimbledon, October 1997

Honours
Football League:
Division One
Champions 1996-97;
Promoted from Division One
(play-offs) 2000-01

Division Two
Champions 1908-09, 1977-78;
Runners-Up 1899-00, 1904-05,1910-11,
1934-35, 1992-93

Division Three
Champions 1972-73

FA Cup:
Winners 1923, 1926, 1929, 1958;
Runners-up 1894, 1904, 1953

Football League Cup:
Runners-up 1995, 2004

Freight Rover Trophy:
Runners-Up 1986

Sherpa Van Trophy:
Winners 1989

Highest at Burnden Park
Overall: 69,912 v Manchester City,
FA Cup 5th Round 18 February 1933
League: 55,477 v Manchester United,
FL1, 1 September 1951

Lowest at Burnden Park
Overall: 1,507 v Rochdale, (Autoglass Trophy)
10 December 1991
League: 2,017 v Sheffield United,
FL1, 2 March 1901

Highest at Reebok Stadium
Overall: 28,353 v Leicester City,
FAPL, 28 December 2003
Premiership: 28,353 v Leicester City,
FAPL, 28 December 2003

Lowest at Reebok Stadium
Overall: 3,673 v Gillingham,
FLC2, 21 September 1999
League: 11,668 v Birmingham City,
FL1, 5 September 1999

Away
Overall: 72,840 v Manchester United,
FL1, 26 March 1948
Premiership: 67,647 v Manchester United,
FAPL, 16 August 2003

Away
Overall: 1,000 v Pisa, Anglo Italian Cup,
16 November 1993; 1,000 v Ascoli,
Anglo Italian Cup, 22 December 1993
League: 1,193 v Newport County, FL3, 4 April 1987

BOLTON WANDERERS POST WAR AVERAGE ATTENDANCES

Season	Average	Season	Average
1946/47	28,700	1975/76	19,390
1947/48	29,408	1976/77	21,794
1948/49	34,113	1977/78	22,877
1949/50	29,788	1978/79	24,772
1950/51	33,152	1979/80	16,359
1951/52	35,832	1980/81	9,847
1952/53	32,066	1981/82	7,597
1953/54	33,739	1982/83	7,512
1954/55	28,418	1983/84	5,892
1955/56	27,964	1984/85	4,951
1956/57	25,219	1985/86	4,846
1957/58	22,029	1986/87	4,851
1958/59	27,659	1987/88	5,017
1959/60	26,978	1988/89	5,705
1960/61	23,827	1989/90	7,286
1961/62	17,519	1990/91	7,279
1962/63	25,180	1991/92	7,867
1963/64	19,755	1992/93	9,062
1964/65	15,739	1993/94	10,498
1965/66	19,968	1994/95	13,029
1966/67	15,176	1995/96	18,822
1967/68	11,487	1996/97	15,820
1968/69	10,536	1997/98	24,352
1969/70	10,041	1998/99	18,201
1970/71	8,414	1999/00	14,244
1971/72	8,173	2000/01	16,062
1972/73	13,928	2001/02	25,098
1973/74	15,942	2002/03	25,017
1974/75	13,799	2003/04	26,795

BOLTON WANDERERS COMPLETE LEAGUE RECORD 1888/89 – 2003/04

Season	League	P	W	D	L	F	A	Pts	Position
1888/89	D1	22	10	2	10	63	59	22	5th
1889/90	D1	22	9	1	12	54	65	19	9th
1890/91	D1	22	12	1	9	47	34	25	5th
1891/92	D1	26	17	2	7	51	37	36	3rd
1892/93	D1	30	13	6	11	56	55	32	5th
1893/94	D1	30	10	4	16	38	52	24	13th
1894/95	D1	30	9	7	14	61	62	25	10th
1895/96	D1	30	16	5	9	49	37	37	4th
1896/97	D1	30	12	6	12	40	36	30	8th
1897/98	D1	30	11	4	15	28	41	26	11th
1898/99	D1	34	9	7	18	37	51	25	17th
1899/00	D2	34	22	10	4	79	25	52	2nd
1900/01	D1	34	13	7	14	39	55	33	10th
1901/02	D1	34	12	8	14	51	56	32	12th
1902/03	D1	34	8	3	23	37	73	19	18th
1903/04	D2	34	12	10	12	59	41	34	7th
1904/05	D2	34	27	2	5	87	32	56	2nd
1905/06	D1	38	17	7	14	81	67	41	6th
1906/07	D1	38	18	8	12	59	47	44	6th
1907/08	D1	38	14	5	19	52	58	33	19th
1908/09	D2	38	24	4	10	59	28	52	1st
1909/10	D1	38	9	6	23	44	71	24	20th
1910/11	D2	38	21	9	8	69	40	51	2nd
1911/12	D1	38	20	3	15	54	43	43	4th
1912/13	D1	38	16	10	12	62	63	42	8th
1913/14	D1	38	16	10	12	65	52	42	6th
1914/15	D1	38	11	8	19	68	84	30	17th
1919/20	D1	42	19	9	14	72	65	47	6th
1920/21	D1	42	19	14	9	77	53	52	3rd
1921/22	D1	42	20	7	15	68	59	47	6th
1922/23	D1	42	14	12	16	50	58	40	13th
1923/24	D1	42	18	14	10	68	34	50	4th
1924/25	D1	42	22	11	9	76	34	55	3rd
1925/26	D1	42	17	10	15	75	76	44	8th
1926/27	D1	42	19	10	13	84	62	48	4th
1927/28	D1	42	16	11	15	81	66	43	7th
1928/29	D1	42	14	12	16	73	80	40	14th
1929/30	D1	42	15	9	18	74	74	39	15th
1930/31	D1	42	15	9	18	68	81	39	14th
1931/32	D1	42	17	4	21	72	80	38	17th
1932/33	D1	42	12	9	21	78	92	33	21st
1933/34	D1	42	21	9	12	79	55	51	3rd
1934/35	D2	42	26	4	12	96	48	56	2nd
1935/36	D1	42	14	13	15	67	76	41	13th
1936/37	D1	42	10	14	18	43	66	34	20th
1937/38	D1	42	15	15	12	64	60	45	7th
1938/39	D1	42	15	15	12	67	58	45	8th
1946/47	D1	42	13	8	21	57	69	34	18th
1947/48	D1	42	16	5	21	46	58	37	17th
1948/49	D1	42	14	10	18	59	68	38	14th
1949/50	D1	42	10	14	18	45	59	34	16th
1950/51	D1	42	19	7	16	64	61	45	8th
1951/52	D1	42	19	10	13	65	61	48	5th

Season	League	P	W	D	L	F	A	Pts	Position
1952/53	D1	42	15	9	18	61	69	39	14th
1953/54	D1	42	18	12	12	75	60	48	5th
1954/55	D1	42	13	13	16	62	69	39	18th
1955/56	D1	42	18	7	17	71	58	43	8th
1956/57	D1	42	16	12	14	65	65	44	9th
1957/58	D1	42	14	10	18	65	87	38	15th
1958/59	D1	42	20	10	12	79	66	50	4th
1959/60	D1	42	20	8	14	59	51	48	6th
1960/61	D1	42	12	11	19	58	73	35	18th
1961/62	D1	42	16	10	16	62	66	42	11th
1962/63	D1	42	15	5	22	55	75	35	18th
1963/64	D1	42	10	8	24	48	80	28	21st
1964/65	D2	42	20	10	12	80	58	50	3rd
1965/66	D2	42	16	9	17	62	59	41	9th
1966/67	D2	42	14	14	14	64	58	42	9th
1967/68	D2	42	13	13	16	60	63	39	12th
1968/69	D2	42	12	14	16	55	67	38	17th
1969/70	D2	42	12	12	18	54	61	36	16th
1970/71	D2	42	7	10	25	35	74	24	22nd
1971/72	D3	46	17	16	13	51	41	50	7th
1972/73	D3	46	25	11	10	73	39	61	1st
1973/74	D2	42	15	12	15	44	40	42	11th
1974/75	D2	42	15	12	15	45	41	42	10th
1975/76	D2	42	20	12	10	64	38	52	4th
1976/77	D2	42	20	11	11	75	54	51	4th
1977/78	D2	42	24	10	8	63	33	58	1st
1978/79	D1	42	12	11	19	54	75	35	17th
1979/80	D1	42	5	15	22	38	73	25	22nd
1980/81	D2	42	14	10	18	61	66	38	18th
1981/82	D2	42	13	7	22	39	61	46	19th
1982/83	D2	42	11	11	20	42	61	44	22nd
1983/84	D3	46	18	10	18	56	60	64	10th
1984/85	D3	46	16	6	24	69	75	54	17th
1985/86	D3	46	15	8	23	54	68	53	18th
1986/87	D3	46	10	15	21	46	58	45	21st
1987/88	D4	46	22	12	12	66	42	78	3rd
1988/89	D3	46	16	16	14	58	54	64	10th
1989/90	D3	46	18	15	13	59	48	69	6th
1990/91	D3	46	24	11	11	64	50	83	4th
1991/92	D3	46	14	17	15	57	56	59	13th
1992/93	D2	46	27	9	10	80	41	90	2nd
1993/94	D1	46	15	14	17	63	64	59	14th
1994/95	D1	46	21	14	11	67	45	77	3rd
1995/96	PL	38	8	5	25	39	71	29	20th
1996/97	D1	46	28	14	4	100	53	98	1st
1997/98	PL	38	9	13	16	41	61	40	18th
1998/99	D1	46	20	16	10	78	59	76	6th
1999/00	D1	46	21	13	12	69	50	76	6th
2000/01	D1	46	24	15	7	76	45	87	3rd
2001/02	PL	38	9	13	16	44	62	40	16th
2002/03	PL	38	10	14	14	41	51	44	17th
2003/04	PL	38	14	11	13	48	56	53	8th

STATS & RECORDS

Biggest Wins
Overall: 13-0 v Sheffield United (H), 01-02-1890, FA Cup Round Two, Pikes Lane
League: 8-0 v Barnsley (H), 06-10-1934, FL2, Burnden Park
Premiership: 5-0 v Leicester City (A), 18-08-2001, Filbert Street

Biggest Defeats
Overall: 1-9 v Preston North End (A), 10-12-1887, FA Cup Round 2
League: 0-7 v Burnley (A) 01-03-1890, FL1, Turf Moor
0-7 v Sheffield Wednesday (A) 01-03-1915, FL1, Hillsborough
0-7 v Manchester City (A) 21-03-1936, FL1, Maine Road
Premiership: 0-6 v Manchester United (H) 25-02-96, Old Trafford

SEASONAL RECORDS

	Overall		Premiership	
Most Wins	**28**	1996-97	**14**	2003-04
Most Home Wins	**18**	1924-25; 1972-73; 1992-93; 1996-97	**7**	1997-98; 2002-03
Most Away Wins	**14**	2000-01	**8**	2003-04
	Overall		Premiership	
Most Defeats	**25**	1970-71; 1995-96	**25**	1995-96
Most Home Defeats	**10**	1909-10; 1963-64; 1970-71; 1986-87; 1995-96	**10**	1995-96
Most Away defeats	**18**	1984-85	**15**	1995-96
	Overall		Premiership	
Most Draws	**17**	1991-92	**14**	2002-03
Most Home Draws	**11**	1979-80	**8**	1997-98; 2002-03; 2003-04
Most Away Draws	**10**	1986-87; 1996-97; 1998-99	**6**	2001-02; 2002-03
	Overall		Premierhsip	
Fewest Wins	**5**	1979-80	**8**	1995-96
Fewest Home Wins	**5**	1979-80; 1995-96; 2001-02	**5**	1995-96; 2001-02
Fewest Away Wins	**0**	1949-50; 1970-71; 1979-80	**2**	1997-98
	Overall		Premiership	
Fewest Defeats	**4**	1899-00; 1996-97	**13**	2003-04
Fewest Home Defeats	**0**	1910-11; 1920-21	**4**	1997-98; 2002-03
Fewest Away Defeats	**3**	1899-00; 1904-05; 1996-97	**8**	2003-04
Fewest Draws	Overall		Premiership	
Fewest Draws	**1**	1889-90; 1890-91	**5**	1995-96
Fewest Home Draws	**0**	1888-89; 1890-91; 1904-05	**4**	1995-96
Fewest Away Draws	**0**	1889-90; 1891-92	**1**	1995-96
	Overall		Premiership	
Most Goals Scored	**100**	1996-97	**48**	2003-04
Most Home Goals Scored	**63**	1934-35	**27**	2002-03
Most Away Goals Scored	40	1996-97	**24**	2001-02; 2003-04
	Overall		Premiership	
Most Goals Conceded	**92**	1932-33	**71**	1995-96
Most Home Goals Conceded	**35**	1952-53; 1957-58; 1963-64	**31**	1995-96; 2001-02
Most Away Goals Conceded	**59**	1932-33	**40**	1995-96
	Overall		Premiership	
Fewest Goals Scored	**28**	1897-98	**39**	1995-96
Fewest Home Goals Scored	**16**	1995-96	**16**	1995-96
Fewest Away Goals Scored	**10**	1897-98	**14**	2002-03
	Overall		Premiership	
Fewest Goals Conceded	**25**	1899-00	**51**	2002-03
Fewest Home Goals Conceded	**7**	1899-00	**21**	2003-04
Fewest Away Goals Conceded	**16**	1904-05	**27**	2002-03

SEQUENCES

League Games Only

Consecutive Wins	**11**	1904-05
Consecutive Defeats	**11**	07-04-1902 – 18-10-1902
Consecutive Draws	**6**	1912-13
Consecutive games unbeaten	**23**	1990-91
Consecutive games without a win	**26**	07-04-1902 – 10-01-1903
Consecutive home wins	**13**	1910-11
Consecutive home defeats	**4**	1902-03
Consecutive away wins	**5**	1904-05; 2000-01
Consecutive away defeats	**11**	1979-80; 1984-85
Consecutive home unbeaten	**21**	1920-21
Consecutive home without a win	**10**	1902-03; 1979-80
Consecutive away unbeaten	**11**	1904-05
Consecutive away without a win	**21**	1979-80
Consecutive without scoring	**5**	1897-98; 1989-90
Consecutive games scoring	**24**	1888-89; 1889-90; 1996-97
Consecutive games conceding	**27**	1901-02; 1902-03

Premiership Only

Consecutive Wins	**5**	2003-04
Consecutive Defeats	**4**	1995-96; 2003-04
Consecutive Draws	**3**	2001-02
Consecutive games unbeaten	**6**	2003-04
Consecutive games without a win	**12**	1997-98; 2001-02
Consecutive home wins	**3**	2002-03
Consecutive home defeats	**3**	1995-96; 2001-02
Consecutive away wins	**3**	1995-96; 2003-04
Consecutive away defeats	**4**	1995-96; 2002-03
Consecutive home unbeaten	**7**	1997-98; 2002-03
Consecutive home without a win	**10**	2001-02
Consecutive away unbeaten	**5**	2001-02
Consecutive away without a win	**17**	1997-98
Consecutive clean sheets	**4**	2003-04
Consecutive without scoring	**2**	2001-02
Consecutive games scoring	**15**	2003-04
Consecutive games conceding	**11**	1995-96; 2001-02

TOP 20 APPEARANCES		
Eddie Hopkinson	**578**	(1956-1970)
Roy Greaves	**567+8**	(1965-80)
Alex Finney	**530**	(1922-1937)
Warwick Rimmer	**521+7**	(1960-1975)
Brian Edwards	**518**	(1950-1965)
Ted Vizard	**512**	(1910-1931)
Nat Lofthouse	**503**	(1946-1961)
Paul Jones	**502**	(1970-1983)
Steve Thompson	**416+6**	(1982-1992)
Roy Hartle	**498+1**	(1952-1966)
Joe Smith	**492**	(1908-1927)
Doug Holden	**463**	(1951-1963)
Billy Butler	**449**	(1921-1933)
Stan Hanson	**423**	(1936-1956)
David Stokes	**420**	(1901-1920)
Fred Hill	**410+2**	(1957-1969)
Syd Farrimond	**403+1**	(1958-1971)
Jimmy Phillips	**390+21**	(1983-2001)
Bert Baverstock	**388**	(1905-1922)
J Seddon =	**375**	(1913-1932)
John Ritson =	**375**	(1967-1978)

TOP 20 GOALSCORERS		
Nat Lofthouse	**285 goals**	503 (1946-61)
Joe Smith	**277**	492 (1908-27)
David Jack	**161**	324 (1920-29)
Jack Milsom	**153**	255 (1929-38)
Ray Westwood	**144**	333 (1930-48)
William Moir	**134**	358 (1946-56)
John Byrom	**130**	340+11 (1996-76)
Harold Blackmore	**122**	165 (1926-32)
Neil Whatmore	**121**	322+16 (1972-84)
John McGinlay	**118**	230+15 (1992-98)
Francis Lee	**106**	210 (1960-68)
James Cassidy	**101**	219 (1889-1898)
Dennis Stevens	**101**	310 (1953-62)
Wattie White	**93**	217 (1902-09)
Albert Shepherd	**90**	123 (1904-09)
John Smith	**87**	174 (1922-28)
Roy Greaves	**85**	567+8 (1965 -80)
George Gibson	**81**	255 (1926-33)
Sam Marsh	**81**	201(1902-12)
Frank Roberts	**80**	168 (1914-23)

These rankings apply to first class fixtures only.

MOST GOALS IN A SINGLE GAME			
5			
T Caldwell	10.09.1983	Walsall, FL3, 8-1	
J Cassidy	01.02.1890	Sheffield W. (h), FA Cup, 13-0	
B Struthers	04.11.1882	Bootle (h), FA Cup, 6-1	
4			
M W Barrass	06.11.1948	Manchester City, (h), FL1, 5-1	
H Blackmore	05.11.1927	Burnley, (h), FL1, 7-0	
	28.12.1929	Everton, (h), FL1, 5-0	
J Cassidy	30.11.1889	Derby County (h), FL1, 7-1	
J Currier	19.02.1944	Southport, (h), FLN, 5-1	
J Henderson	01.01.1895	Derby County, (h), FL1, 6-0	
J Hunt	11.01.1940	Oldham Athletic (a), FLN, 5-3	
	16.01.1943	Oldham Athletic, (h), FLN, 5-0	

4 cont.			
D Jack	22.04.1925	Blackburn Rovers, (h), FL1, 6-0	
N Lofthouse	10.02.1945	Tranmere Rovers, (h), FLN, 6-1	
	07.04.1945	Blackpool, (a), FLN, 4-1	
	10.12.1955	Birmingham City, (h), FL1, 6-0	
J Milsom	30.12.1933	West Ham United, (h), FL2, 5-1	
	02.01.1935	Burnley, (h), FL2, 7-0	
W Moir	30.08.1948	Aston Villa, (a), FL1, 4-2	
	27.12.1948	Sheffield United, (h), FL1, 6-1	
A Shepherd	18.11.1905	Nottingham Forest, (h), FL1, 6-0	
D Weir	18.01.1890	Belfast Distillery, (h), FA Cup, 10-2	
R Westwood	06.10.1934	Barnsley, (h), FL2, 8-0	

Sam **Allaardyce**

Date of Birth **19-10-1954**
Place of Birth **Dudley, England**
Position **Manager**
Date Appointed **19-10-99**
Previous Clubs Managed **Notts County, Blackpool, Limerick (Ire)**

MANAGERIAL CAREER

Club	From	To	Games	Won	Lost	Drawn
Bolton	19-10-99	Present	232	93	70	69
Notts County	16-01-97	14-10-99	147	56	50	41
Blackpool	19-07-94	29-05-96	102	44	35	23
Totals			**481**	**193**	**155**	**133**

Managerial Career

Last season, Sam Allardyce took Bolton to their highest placing in 44 years, when the team finished eighth in the Premiership.

He is now regarded as one of the Club's greatest ever managers.

Sam Allardyce's men have rewritten the record books and created a piece of history during the 2003/04 season.

The team equalled its best away record ever in the top flight with eight wins.

They also recorded five successive league victories in the top flight, which is the first time it has been achieved since 1927/28 season and for the first time for 40 years the Club will spend four successive seasons in the top flight.

Big Sam returned 'home' on his birthday in October 1999, after leaving Notts County, to manage the club he signed for as a 15 year-old in 1969. In his first season at the Reebok Stadium, he guided Wanderers to the semi-finals of the FA Cup, League Cup and the First Division Play-Offs.

The following season, Wanderers put the abject disappointment of the previous season's play-off defeat behind them to record an emphatic 3-0 victory over Preston North End in the First Division Play-Off Final at Cardiff's Millennium Stadium. That result earned Wanderers promotion to the Premiership for the first time since 1997 and enabled Big Sam to realise his lifelong ambition of managing the Wanderers in the Premiership.

He commenced his coaching career in football in his native West Midlands with West Bromwich Albion whilst still playing for The Baggies. He then became Assistant Manager at Preston North End and Sunderland.

He became manager of Limerick in Ireland before taking charge at Blackpool. Whilst at Bloomfield Road he took The Tangerines to the 1996 Second Division play-off final. In 1997 he took charge of Notts County and won the Third Division Championship in 1998.

Playing Career

15 year-old Sam Allardyce arrived at Burnden Park in 1969 and turned professional with the Wanderers in November 1973. He made his league debut in November 1973 and was a regular member of the successful Wanderers sides in the mid 1970s who twice narrowly missed out on promotion to the old First Division. In 1978 he won a Second Division Championship medal with Bolton.

After a total of 214 first class games he left the Wanderers to join Sunderland in 1980 for a fee of £150,000.

When his spell at Roker Park came to an end he then played for Millwall, Tampa Bay Rowdies, Coventry City and Huddersfield Town before returning to Burnden Park for another spell in 1985. He only managed 17 appearances in his one season back in Bolton and then joined neighbours Preston North End where he helped them to win promotion from the old Fourth Division in 1987.

PLAYING CAREER			
Club	Date Joined	League Apps	Goals
Bolton	01-11-71	180+4	21
Sunderland	01-07-80	24+1	2
Millwall	01-09-81	63+0	2
Coventry City	01-09-83	28+0	1
Huddsfield Town	01-07-84	37+0	0
Bolton	01-07-85	14+0	0
Preston North End	01-08-86	88+2	2
WBA	01-06-89	0+1	0
Preston North End	01-08-92	1+2	0
Totals		435+10	28

Phil **Brown**

Phil **Brown**

Date of Birth **30-05-59**
Place of Birth **South Shields, England**
Position **Assistant Manager**
Date Appointed **June 1996**

Bolton Career

Phil Brown became Sam Allardyce's right-hand man at Blackpool after joining them as a player from the Wanderers in 1994. He came back to Burnden Park at the start of the 1996-1997 season as First Team Coach under then manager Colin Todd and helped the Club to their fantastic Championship winning campaign culminating in their second appearance in the Premiership.

Following Todd's departure in 1999, Phil had a brief spell as caretaker-manager before linking up again with Big Sam where they remained a successful double-act ever since.

Career

Phil turned professional with Hartlepool United in July 1978 and went on to make 217 appearances before joining Halifax Town in July 1985. Whilst at The Shay he clocked up 135 league games before crossing the Pennines to join the Wanderers in June 1988.

He captained the Wanderers to Wembley success in the Sherpa Van Trophy in 1989 and also to promotion from the old Second Division in 1993. During this spell he clocked up an amazing 171 consecutive appearances for the Club. In total, he registered 332 first class games for Bolton Wanderers and in 1994 he ended his playing career with Blackpool.

PLAYING CAREER

Club	From	To	League Apps	League Goals	FA Cup Apps	FA Cup Goals	League Cup Apps	League Cup Goals	Other Apps	Other Goals
Blackpool	July 94	May 96	33+11	5	2+2	0	2+0	1	2+1	0
Bolton	June 88	July 94	254+4	14	23+0	1	25+0	1	28+0	1
Halifax	July 85	June 88	135+0	19	8+0	1	6+0	1	9+0	0
Hartlepool	July 78	July 85	210+7	8	11+0	0	12+0	0	3+0	1
Totals			632+22	46	44+2	2	45+0	3	42+1	2

Anthony **Barness**

Anthony **Barness**

Date of Birth **25-02-1973**
Place of Birth **Lewisham, England**
Position **Defender**
Nationality **England**
Signed On **04-07-00**
Bolton Debut **v Burnley, 12-08-00, FL1, Reebok Stadium, D 1-1**

Bolton Career
Since his arrival in July 2000 from Charlton Athletic, Anthony has made over 70 appearances for Bolton Wanderers. Capable of playing in either full-back role, he is more accustomed to playing at right-back and, when needed, can switch to the centre.

Last season, Anthony figured in 15 matches to help Wanderers record their best finish for 44 years.

Career
He started his career with Charlton as a trainee before turning professional in March 1991 and then had spells at Chelsea, Middlesbrough and Southend United before returning to The Addicks.

PLAYING CAREER										
Club			League		FA Cup		League Cup		Other	
	From	To	Apps	Goals	Apps	Goals	Apps	Goals	Apps	Goals
Bolton	Jul 00		68+17		7		8+2		3	
Charlton	Aug 96	Jul 00	83+13	3	3+1		5		1+1	
Southend (Loan)	Feb 96	Mar 96	5							
Middlesbrough (Loan)	Aug 93	Aug 93							1	
Chelsea	Sep 92	Aug 96	12+2				2		2+1	
Charlton	Mar 91	Sep 92	21+6	1	3		2		1+1	1
Totals			189+38	4	13+1		17+2		8+3	1

Michael **Bridges**

Michael **Bridges**

Date of Birth **05-08-1978**
Place of Birth **North Shields, England**
Position **Forward**
Nationality **England**
Signed On **01-07-04**
Honours **U21**

Bolton Career

Signed for the Wanderers in summer on an initial one-year contract. His arrival at the Reebok Stadium will see him link-up with Sam Allardyce for the second time in his career, after receiving several coaching sessions from the Wanderers boss earlier in his career.

The 25 year old marksmen is keen to follow in the footsteps of Kevin Davies by resurrecting his career at the Reebok Stadium

Career

Michael Bridges arrived at Elland Road in a £5 million deal from Sunderland at the beginning of 1999/00, after growing frustrated with his inability to break into the first team ahead of Niall Quinn and Kevin Phillips. He quickly established himself as a fans' favourite with a hat trick in only his second appearance in a Leeds shirt.

The young striker - a native of the North East - was determined to join Leeds United because of David O'Leary's youth policy, ironically turning down a move to link up with former Leeds boss, George Graham, at Tottenham Hotspur.

He was soon turning in some impressive performances, and proved a vital addition to the squad with his ability to hold the ball up and deceptive turn of pace. Bridges went on to score over 20 goals in his first season at Elland Road and was a key player for Leeds in their European campaign. His reward was to become a regular in the England under-21 squad, and started the opening match of the European Championships against Slovakia.

Injury robbed Bridges of taking part in Leeds' historic Champions League run in 2000/01, and he was once again out of most of 2001/02, but make his comeback in Gary Kelly's testimonial in May 2002.

Bridges played in nine games at the start of the 2002/03 season but injury has once again forced him to sit on the sidelines. He managed a few more appearances in 2003/04, and in January 2004 he joined Newcastle United on loan for three months.

PLAYING CAREER

Club	From	To	League Apps	League Goals	FA Cup Apps	FA Cup Goals	League Cup Apps	League Cup Goals	Other Apps	Other Goals
Bolton	Jul 04									
Newcastle (Loan)	Feb 04	May 04	0+6						1+2	
Leeds	Jul 99	May 04	40+16	19	1+1		3+2		17+2	2
Sunderland	Nov 95	Jul 99	31+48	16	2		8+3	5		
Totals			71+70	35	3+1		11+5	5	18+4	2

Ivan **Campo**

Ivan **Campo**

Date of Birth **21-02-1974**
Place of Birth **San Sebastian, Spain**
Position **Defender**
Nationality **Spain**
Signed On **31-08-02**
Honours **Full**
Bolton Debut **v Manchester United,
11-09-02, FAPL, Old Trafford, W 1-0**

Bolton Career

Ivan Campo initially joined the club on a season-long loan deal on 31 August, 2002 – the transfer deadline day!

Sam Allardyce's perseverance finally paid off when the central-defender agreed the move, marking the successful conclusion to one of the longest transfer sagas in the Club's history.

He arrived as a central-defender but made a more than successful conversion to midfield – a position he made his own. He scored on his home debut – as a substitute in the home defeat against Liverpool and also found the net in a 2-0 win against Manchester City.

After the expiration of his loan at the end of the 2002/03 season, he signed a two-year deal to become a permanent member of Big Sam's playing staff.

Last term he was ever present in the Premiership scoring four goals in 38 appearances.

Career

The Spaniard spent four seasons with Real Madrid notching up 60 appearances in La Liga. Prior to his arrival at the Santiago Bernabeu, Campo played for Real Mallorca, Valencia, Valladolid and Deportivo Alavés. He has earned extensive experience in Europe and has won four international caps for Spain, his last appearance coming in a 4-1 defeat against Germany in August 2000.

PLAYING CAREER										
Club			League		FA Cup		League Cup		Other	
	From	To	Apps	Goals	Apps	Goals	Apps	Goals	Apps	Goals
Bolton	Aug 02		65+4	6	2		7			
Totals			65+4	6	2		7			

Previous Clubs

Real Madrid (Jul 98 – Aug 02), Mallorca (Jul 97 – Jul 98), Valencia (Jul 96 – Jun 98), Valladolid (Nov 95 – Jun 96), Alaves (Jul 93 – Nov 95)

Ricardo **Vaz Te**

Ricardo **Vaz Te**

Date of Birth **01-10-86**
Place of Birth **Lisbon, Portugal**
Position **Striker**
Nationality **Portugal**
Signed On **July 2003**
Bolton Debut: **v Tranmere Rovers, 03-01-04, FA3, Prenton Park, D 1-1**
Honours **U17**

Career

Ricardo was courted by the giants of Portuguese football before opting to join Wanderers. A prolific marksman, Ricardo made an immediate impact in his first three games for the Academy side last season netting eight goals.

He made his first team debut in the FA Cup tie against Tranmere Rovers at Prenton Park in January 2004. He lists Thierry Henry as his favourite player. He made his Premiership debut against Middlesbrough last season when he came on as substitute.

Ricardo has represented Portugal at under 17 level.

PLAYING CAREER										
Club			League		FA Cup		League Cup		Other	
	From	To	Apps	Goals	Apps	Goals	Apps	Goals	Apps	Goals
Bolton	Jul 03		0+1		1+1					
Totals			0+1		1+1					

Kevin **Davies**

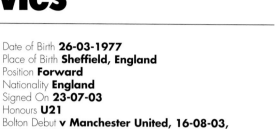

Kevin **Davies**

Date of Birth **26-03-1977**
Place of Birth **Sheffield, England**
Position **Forward**
Nationality **England**
Signed On **23-07-03**
Honours **U21**
Bolton Debut **v Manchester United, 16-08-03,
FAPL, Old Trafford, L 4-0**

Bolton Career

Kevin signed a one-year deal after impressing Sam Allardyce during a trial spell in the summer of 2003.

Kevin was released by Southampton at the end of the 2002/2003 season. He made his Wanderers debut in the 4-0 reverse at Old Trafford on the opening day of the season.

He was voted Wanderers' best player in 2003/04, by his peers, and proved to be a real handful for defences up and down the country with his no nonsense approach.

Davies was one of only three Bolton players ever present in the Premiership last term scoring nine goals.

Career

Kevin shot to fame as a youngster with Chesterfield in the mid to late 1990s. He scored a memorable hattrick for the Spireites against Wanderers at Burnden Park during the club's shock run to the FA Cup semi-finals in 1997.

Southampton purchased him from Saltergate before Blackburn Rovers splashed out £7 million for his services. He returned to the south coast after his spell in Lancashire didn't work out.

PLAYING CAREER

Club	From	To	League Apps	League Goals	FA Cup Apps	FA Cup Goals	League Cup Apps	League Cup Goals	Other Apps	Other Goals
Bolton	Jul 03		38	9			4+1	1		
Millwall (Loan)	Sep 02	Nov 02	6+3	3						
Southampton	Aug 99	Jul 03	59+23	10	3+5	2	3+2	1		
Blackburn	Jun 98	Aug 99	12+12	1	2	1	3		1	
Southampton	May 97	Jun98	20+5	9	1		3+1	3		
Chesterfield	Apr 94	May 97	113+16	22	10	6	7+2	1	9+2	1
Totals			248+59	54	16+5	9	20+6	6	10+2	1

Les **Ferdinand**

Les **Ferdinand**

Date of Birth **08-012-66**
Place of Birth **Acton, England**
Position **Forward**
Nationality **England**
Signed On **05-07-04**
Honours **Full**

Bolton Career

Les Ferdinand became a Bolton Wanderers player in the summer when he signed a one-year deal.
The 37 year-old became Sam Allardyce's second signing following the arrival of Michael Bridges.

Career

The striker decided to remain in the Premiership despite being offered a new deal by relegated Leicester City, for whom he netted 12 goals in 28 games last season.
The Acton born frontman made his name with Queens Park Rangers in the late 1980s before joining Newcastle United in 1995 for a fee of £6 million.
Spurs paid the same amount to take him back to London in 1997, where he spent just under six seasons. A six-month spell at West Ham was followed by his stint at Leicester City.
He also won 17 caps for England, scoring five goals.
Ferdinand has been a thorn in Wanderers' side in recent seasons. Last term, he netted in both league encounters against the Foxes, whilst at Spurs, in 2001, he bagged a memorable nine-minute hattrick in a league cup encounter at White Hart Lane.
Immensely strong in the air, Les is also a powerful and forceful runner who possesses a good touch despite his muscular physique.

PLAYING CAREER

Club	From	To	League Apps	League Goals	FA Cup Apps	FA Cup Goals	League Cup Apps	League Cup Goals	Other Apps	Other Goals
Bolton	Jul 04									
Leicester City	Jul 03	Jul 04	20+9	12	1+1	1				
West Ham United	Jan 03	Jul 03	12+2	2						
Tottenham Hotspur	Jul 97	Jan 03	97+21	33	15+1	1	11+4	5		
Newcastle United	Jul 95	Jul 97	67+1	41	4+1	2	6	3	5	4
Brentford	Mar 88	May 88	3							
QPR	Mar 87	Jul 95	152+11	80	6+1	3	11+2	7	1	
Totals	**351+44**	**168**	**26+4**	**7**	**28+6**	**15**	**6**	**4**		

Previous Clubs

Besiktas (Mar 88 - Jun 88), Hayes (Aug 87 - Mar 88)

Ricardo **Gardner**

Ricardo **Gardner**

Date of Birth **25-09-78**
Place of Birth **St Andrews, Jamaica**
Position **Midfielder**
Nationality **Jamaica**
Signed On **01-07-98**
Honours **Full, U21, Yth**
Bolton Debut **v Hartlepool United, 25-08-98,
LC1, Victoria Park, L 0-3**

Bolton Career
Ricardo was 19 years old when he came to international prominence in the World Cup of 1998 with Jamaica. Colin Todd acted swiftly and signed the Reggae Boy for a £1 million fee from Harbour View.

His league debut saw him come on as a substitute against West Bromwich Albion and score a late goal as Wanderers ran out 3-2 winner. He suffered a cruciate ligament injury in February 2000 which kept him sidelined until the October of the following season.

The winger, who is one of the club's longest-serving current players, has featured in more than 150 games for Wanderers and has scored 21 goals in all competitions.

Last season was cut short, when the Jamaican international sustained knee ligament damage in the home match against Manchester United in Jan 2004.

Career
Ricardo featured in the World Cup of 1998 with Jamaica and in total has won more than 20 caps for the Reggae Boyz.

PLAYING CAREER										
Club			League		FA Cup		League Cup		Other	
	From	To	Apps	Goals	Apps	Goals	Apps	Goals	Apps	Goals
Bolton	Jul 88		152+24	15	6+3		13+4	2	6	2
Totals			152+24	15	6+3		13+4	2	6	2

Previous Clubs
Harbour View (Aug 97 – Jul 98)

Nicky **Hunt**

Nicky **Hunt**

Date of Birth **03-09-1983**
Place of Birth **Bolton, England**
Position **Defender**
Nationality **England**
Signed On **01-08-00**
Honours **U21**
Bolton Debut **v Sheffield United, 06-05-01,**
FL1, Reebok Stadium, D 1-1

Bolton Career
Nicky made his Premiership debut against Manchester United on the opening day of season 2003/2004 – although he made his firstteam debut two seasons earlier as a 17 year-old. He came on as a substitute for Colin Hendry in the final home league game of the 2000/2001 season against Sheffield United.

Nicky signed professional forms with the Club in the summer of 2003.

Last season he burst onto the scene with some impressive performances, which saw he make 28 starts in the Premiership and he has firmly made the right back role his own at the Reebok.

The Westhoughton born defender, made such an impact in the first team that he made his England under 21 debut in a 3-2 win against Holland at Hull in February 2004.

He has pace, tenacity and is a great distributor of the ball and will be a real force in the Barclays Premiership this season.

In the Summer of 2004, he signed a new extension to his contract which will see him at the Reebok until June 2008.

PLAYING CAREER										
Club			League		FA Cup		League Cup		Other	
	From	To	Apps	Goals	Apps	Goals	Apps	Goals	Apps	Goals
Bolton	Aug 00		28+4	1	2+1		6			
Totals			28+4	1	2+1		6			

Jussi **Jaaskelainen**

Jussi **Jaaskelainen**

Date of Birth **19-04-1975**
Place of Birth **Mikkeli, Finland**
Position **Goalkeeper**
Nationality **Finland**
Signed On **11-11-97**
Honours **Full, U21; Yth**
Bolton Debut **v Crystal Palace, 08-08-98, FL1, Selhurst Park, D 2-2**

Bolton Career

Acknowledged as one of the best custodians in the Premiership, Jussi has made over 200 first-team appearances for Wanderers.

He was an ever-present in last season's league campaign and even found time to play for Finland on several occasions.

He suffered a cruciate ligament injury during the promotion winning campaign of 2000/2001 but returned to star between the posts the following season. So much so, he was voted as the best goalkeeper upon Wanderers' return to Premiership - during a joint poll between Sky Sports and Barclaycard.

He arrived at the club in 1997 from Finnish club VPS Vaasa.

Jaaskelainen won the Club's Lion of Vienna Award last season for outstanding service to the Wanderers.

Career

Jussi has won over ten caps for Finland, since making his debut against Malta in 1998, and has also played for the Finnish Under 21s. He started his career with hometown club MP Mikkelin in 1994 before signing for VPS Vaasa in 1996.

PLAYING CAREER										
Club			League		FA Cup		League Cup		Other	
	From	To	Apps	Goals	Apps	Goals	Apps	Goals	Apps	Goals
Bolton	Nov 97		**204+1**		**5**		**13**		**2**	
Totals			**204+1**		**5**		**13**		**2**	

Previous Clubs

VPS Vassa (Aug 96 – Nov 97), MP Mikkelin May 94 – May 95)

Radhi **Jaidi**

Radhi **Jaidi**

Date of Birth **30-08-1975**
Place of Birth **Tunis, Tunisia**
Position **Defender**
Nationality **Tunisia**
Signed On **Jul 2004**

Career

Radhi Jaidi made the transition from the Tunisian League to the English Premiership on the 1st of July when he signed a two-year deal with Bolton Wanderers Football Club.

The 6ft 4ins central defender, who starred in his country's campaign to win the African Cup of Nations earlier this year, has won eight Tunisian championships with Esperance de Tunis.

The 28 year old is a highly experienced international, picking up 69 caps for his country.

PLAYING CAREER										
Club			League		FA Cup		League Cup		Other	
	From	To	Apps	Goals	Apps	Goals	Apps	Goals	Apps	Goals
Bolton	Jul 04									
Totals										

Previous Clubs

Esperance de Tunis (Jun 92 – Jul 04)

Florent **Laville**

Florent **Laville**

Date of Birth **07-08-1973**
Place of Birth **Lyon, France**
Position **Defender**
Nationality **France**
Signed On **02-07-03**
Bolton Debut **v Manchester United, 22-02-03,
FAPL, Reebok Stadium, D 1-1**

Bolton Career

Florent Laville became Sam Allardyce's number one target at the start of last season after the central defender helped the defence to keep six clean-sheets in their last ten games of the 2002/03 - whilst on loan from Lyon.

He initially arrived at the Reebok Stadium on last day of January 2003 - the day the transfer window closed - from reigning French champions, Lyon, where he acquired vast experience in Le Championat. He has also played in the Champions League.

Much to the delight of Wanderers fans, 'The Rock' became a permanent member of the playing staff when he signed a two-year contract in the summer of 2003.

Last season was cut short when he sustained knee ligament damage in the 2-0 victory over Middlesbrough at the Reebok in September 2003.

PLAYING CAREER										
Club			League		FA Cup		League Cup		Other	
	From	To	Apps	Goals	Apps	Goals	Apps	Goals	Apps	Goals
Bolton	Jan 03		15							
Totals			**15**							

Previous Clubs

Lyon (Aug 98 – Jul 03)

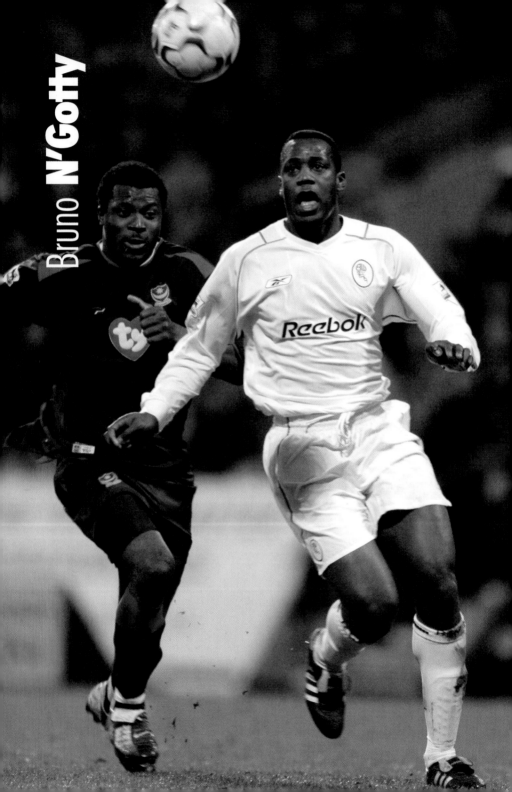
Bruno **N'Gotty**

Bruno **N'Gotty**

Date of Birth **10-06-71**
Place of Birth **Lyon, France**
Position **Defender**
Nationality **French**
Signed On **28-01-2002**
Honours **Full**
Bolton Debut **v Blackburn Rovers, 19-10-01,
FAPL, Ewood Park, D 1-1**

Bolton Career
Bruno N'Gotty initially came to the Reebok Stadium on loan from French club, Marseille, in September 2001. He made his debut as a substitute in the 1-1 draw against Blackburn Rovers at Ewood Park that month.

After a string of impressive performances his loan deal became permanent in January 2002. Last season, the Frenchman was at his imperious best in the central defensive role. He played 33 games and scored three crucial goals from close-range.

The former French international signed a two-year deal in the summer, which will keep him at the Club until June 2006.

Career
Frenchman Bruno signed for his hometown club – Lyon – in August 1988. He amassed well over 200 games for them before joining Paris St Germain in 1995.

He scored the winning goal for PSG in the 1996 Cup Winners Cup final.

After notching over 80 games for the French outfit he crossed the border to Italy to sign for AC Milan in 1998. He was then loaned out to Venezia and played in 16 league games before returning to France with Marseille in the summer of 2001. He has represented his country on six occasions.

PLAYING CAREER										
Club			League		FA Cup		League Cup		Other	
	From	To	Apps	Goals	Apps	Goals	Apps	Goals	Apps	Goals
Bolton	Jan 02		67+1	5	1		6			
Bolton (Loan)	Sep 01	Jan 02	12+2				2+1			
Totals			**79+3**	**5**	**1**		**8+1**			

Previous Clubs
Marseille (Sep 01 – Sep 02), Venezia (Aug 99 – Dec 99), AC Milan (Aug 98 – Jan 00), Paris St-Germain (Aug 95 – Aug 98), Lyon (May 95 – Aug 98)

Kevin **Nolan**

Kevin **Nolan**

Date of Birth **24-06-82**
Place of Birth **Liverpool, England**
Position **Midfielder**
Nationality **England**
Signed On **01-08-99**
Honours **U21, U20, Yth**
Bolton Debut **v Charlton Athletic, 04-03-00,
FL1, Reebok Stadium, L 0-2**

Bolton Career

Kevin Nolan had one of his best seasons for the Wanderers. The Liverpool born midfielder recorded 37 out of a possible 38 Premiership games, last season, scoring nine goals in the league. He recorded 12 goals in total, which made him the leading goalscorer at the Reebok Stadium,

The 22 year old former Bolton youth star has not only took Bolton Wanderers by storm but also the nation and emerged as one of the brightest young stars in the game.

A product of the Wanderers Academy, he made his first team debut as a 17 year-old in a 2-0 defeat against Charlton Athletic at the Reebok Stadium in March 2000.

In the 2001/2002 season he ended up as Wanderers' second highest goalscorer with eight vital strikes and also managed to captain the side when they played Liverpool at Anfield on New Year's Day.

He has made over 140 appearances for the club.

Career

Kevin was spotted player for Liverpool Schoolboys before being snapped up by the Academy as a 15 year-old. Whilst at the Reebok, Kevin has represented England at Under 18 and Under 20 levels and made the step-up to the Under 21s under David Platt last term.

PLAYING CAREER										
Club			League		FA Cup		League Cup		Other	
	From	To	Apps	Goals	Apps	Goals	Apps	Goals	Apps	Goals
Bolton	Aug 99		111+29	19	5+5	3	5+3	2	2	
Totals			111+29	19	5+5	3	5+3	2	2	

Jay-Jay **Okocha**

Reebok

Jay-Jay **Okocha**

Date of Birth **14-08-73**
Place of Birth **Enugu, Nigeria**
Position **Midfielder**
Nationality **Nigeria**
Signed On **18-06-02**
Bolton Debut **v Fulham, 17-08-02,**
FAPL, Loftus Road, L 1-4

Bolton Career

Wanderers' skipper Jay Jay Okocha committed his long term future to Bolton Wanderers by signing a new three-year contract in May 2004.

Okocha became Sam Allardyce's first summer signing of the 2002/2003 season when he arrived at the Reebok Stadium on a free transfer from Paris St Germain.

The Nigerian midfielder signed a two-year contract just days after starring for Nigeria in the World Cup finals in Japan and South Korea.

Although he got his debut season off to a slow start, Okocha found top gear towards the second part of that campaign. With spectacular goals – to become the joint-top scorer for Wanderers – and a vast array of mesmerising tricks, the Nigerian soon garnered high-profile attention as he helped Wanderers to avoid relegation.

Last season he failed to score in the Premiership from 33 starts, but scored three crucial goals in Wanderers' run to the Carling Cup Final.

Career

The 28 year-old became a free agent after deciding not to renew his contract with Paris St Germain where he was the club's recording signing after arriving from Turkish outfit Fenerbahçe for £10 million in 1998.

Whilst in Turkey, Jay-Jay hit 30 league goals in just two seasons before his big money transfer to France.

He also played for Eintracht Frankfurt in the German League between 1992 and 1996.

He captained the Super Eagles during their three matches in the 2002 World Cup and made history by becoming the first Nigerian to play in three World Cup Finals when they took on Argentina in the opening Group F clash.

In 1996, he won a gold medal when Nigeria became the first African team to win the Olympic tournament.

He also captained Nigeria in the 2003 African Cup Of Nations Tournament.

Although he withdrew his resignation from appearing in international football, he has since confirmed that he'll only play in competitive matches for the Super Eagles.

PLAYING CAREER										
Club			League		FA Cup		League Cup		Other	
	From	To	Apps	Goals	Apps	Goals	Apps	Goals	Apps	Goals
Bolton	Jun 02		59+7	7	0+1		5+1	3		
Totals			59+7	7	0+1		5+1	3		

Previous Clubs

PSG (Aug 98 – Jun 02), Fenerbache (Aug 96 – May 98), Eintract Frankfurt (Aug 92 – May 98)

Henrik **Pedersen**

Henrik **Pedersen**

Date of Birth **10-06-1975**
Place of Birth **Jutland, Denmark**
Position **Forward**
Nationality **Denmark**
Signed On **03-07-01**
Honours **Full**
Bolton Debut **v Leicester City, 18-08-01,
FAPL, Filbert Street, W 5-0**

Bolton Career

Henrik was one of Big Sam's first Premiership signings for the club when he arrived from Danish Super-League outfit Silkeborg for £650,000 in the summer of 2001. Wanderers fought off competition from the likes of Borussia Dortmund and VfB Stuttgart for the striker's signature.

He made his debut for the Wanderers, coming on as a substitute, against Leicester City in the opening day demolition. His first goal for his new club came against Walsall in the Worthington Cup during September 2001.

Last season was his best yet in a Wanderers shirt, when he scored seven goals from 19 starts in the Premiership.

Career

In his final season with Silkeborg, Henrik notched 25 goals in 33 appearances as they qualified for European football. He was a prolific marksmen in Denmark, netting 62 goals in 122 appearances for his only club.

Henrik has won one cap for the Danish national team in a friendly against Faroe Islands in August 2000.

PLAYING CAREER										
Club			League		FA Cup		League Cup		Other	
	From	To	Apps	Goals	Apps	Goals	Apps	Goals	Apps	Goals
Bolton	Jul 01		55+22	14	4	1	5+5	3		
Totals			55+22	14	4	1	5+5	3		

Previous Clubs

Silkeborg (Apr 02 – May 02), Silkeborg (Aug 95- Jul 01)

Kevin **Poole**

Kevin **Poole**

Date of Birth **21-07-1963**
Place of Birth **Bromsgrove, England**
Position **Goalkeeper**
Nationality **England**
Signed On **26-10-2001**
Bolton Debut **v Everton, 03-11-01,**
FAPL, Reebok Stadium, D 2-2

Bolton Career

Kevin came to the Reebok Stadium in October 2001 as emergency cover for Jussi Jaaskelainen and Steve Banks after being released from his contract at Birmingham City. He didn't have to wait too long for his debut. During the pre-match warm-up against Everton on 3 November, 2001, Jaaskelainen sustained an injury which prevented him from standing in between the posts.

Poole suddenly found himself in the starting line-up and, despite conceding two goals, produced a great display in the goals for the Wanderers.

Although he didn't feature last term, Kevin signed a new one-year contract to keep him at the Reebok Stadium until the end of this season.

Now in his 41st year, Kevin is still as fit and active as his peers and will continue to provide quality back-up as cover for Jaaskelainen. He is now the oldest player in the Barclays Premiership.

Career

Bromsgrove-born Kevin, began his career with hometown club Aston Villa in 1981. During his time at Villa Park he was loaned out to Northampton Town and played in three league games. After making 28 appearances for Villa he joined Middlesbrough in 1987.

Again he was loaned out – this time to Hartlepool – where he made 12 league appearances. A £40,000 fee saw him switch Ayresome Park for Filbert Street were he made his name as Leicester City's goalkeeper. Six years and over 160 appearances later he joined another Midlands club – Birmingham City – where he played in just over 150 games.

PLAYING CAREER										
Club			League		FA Cup		League Cup		Other	
	From	To	Apps	Goals	Apps	Goals	Apps	Goals	Apps	Goals
Bolton	Oct 01		3		4		5			
Birmingham	Aug 97	Oct 01	55		2		7		3	
Leicester	Jul 91	May 97	163		8		10		13	
Hartlepool	Mar 91	May 91	12							
Middlesbro	Aug 87	Jul 91	34		2		4		2	
Northampton	Nov 84	Dec 84	3							
Aston Villa	Jun 81	Aug 87	29		1		2		1	
Totals			**299**		**17**		**28**		**19**	

Stelios

Stelios

Date of Birth **12-07-1974**
Place of Birth **Athens, Greece**
Position **Midfielder**
Nationality **Greece**
Signed On **30-05-03**
Honours **Full**
Bolton Debut **v Manchester United, 16-08-03, FAPL, Old Trafford L 4-0**

Bolton Career

Stelios signed for the Wanderers in the spring of 2003, when he arrived from Greek champions Olympiakos.

During his first season in England, the Greek international made over 30 appearances and was on the scoresheet three times. Stelios, who arguably has the longest surname in the Premiership (Giannakopoulos), is an attack-minded midfielder offering quick feet and neat skills on the right.

Career

Stelios won seven Greek championships with Olympiakos and was the mainstay of their successful teams. However, he felt the time was right in his career to have a spell in the Premiership and Wanderers were lucky enough to obtain his signature.

He has extensive Champions League experience and has won over 20 caps for his country.

In the Summer of 2004 Stelios was in the Greek starting line-up which, against all odds, won the European Championships in Portugal.

PLAYING CAREER										
Club			League		FA Cup		League Cup		Other	
	From	To	Apps	Goals	Apps	Goals	Apps	Goals	Apps	Goals
Bolton	May 03		17+14	2	2		4+2	2		
Totals			17+14	2	2		4+2	2		

Previous Clubs

Olympiakos (Jun 96 – May 03), Paniliakos (Jun 93 – May 96), Ethnikos Asteras (Jun 92 - May 93)

Premiership Guide

 # Arsenal

Useful Information
Website: www.arsenal.com
Address: Arsenal Stadium, Avenell Road, Highbury, London N5 1BU
Main Switchboard: 020 7704 4000

Travel Information
Car Parking: Parking near the ground is difficult as restrictions come into force.
By Train: The nearest stations are Finsbury Park (approx 10 minutes walk) and Highbury & Islington (approx 20 minutes walk).
By Tube: Arsenal is the nearest tube station (situated on the Piccadilly Line).
By Bus: Numbers 4, 19 and 236 go to Blackstock Road, the ground is approximately 10 minute walk.

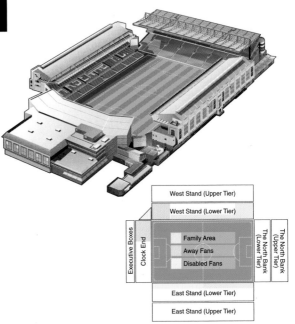

STATISTICS

Final Standings 03-04

Pos		W	D	L	Pts
1	Arsenal	26	12	0	90
2	Chelsea	24	7	7	79
3	Man Utd	23	6	9	75

All-Time Record
League matches only (home and away)

Played	Won
102	**31**

Drawn	Lost
29	**42**

Last Five Meetings

20/03/2004 Premiership
Arsenal 2-1 Bolton Wanderers
Scorer: Campo 41

20/12/2003 Premiership
Bolton Wanderers 1-1 Arsenal
Scorer: Pedersen 83

26/04/2003 Premiership
Bolton Wanderers 2-2 Arsenal
Scorers: Djorkaeff 74, Keown 84 (og)

21/09/2002 Premiership
Arsenal 2-1 Bolton Wanderers
Scorer: Farrelly 47

29/04/2002 Premiership
Bolton Wanderers 0-2 Arsenal

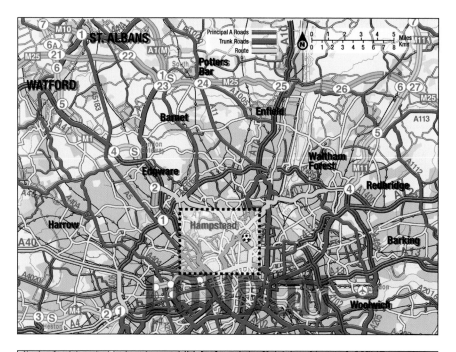

Aston Villa

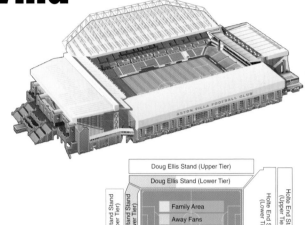

Useful Information
Website: www.avfc.co.uk
Address: Villa Park, Trinity Road,
Birmingham, B6 6HE
Main Switchboard: 0121 327 2299

Travel Information
By Train: It is a two minute walk to Villa
Park from Witton Station. Aston Station is a
10 minute walk. Connecting trains run from
Birmingham New Street.
By Bus: The number 7 runs from
Birmingham City Centre directly to the
ground. Numbers 11a and 11c also serve
the ground.

Doug Ellis Stand (Upper Tier)

Doug Ellis Stand (Lower Tier)

North Stand Stand (Upper Tier)

North Stand Stand (Lower Tier)

Family Area

Away Fans

Disabled Fans

Holte End Stand (Lower Tier)

Holte End Stand (Upper Tier)

Trinity Road Stand (Lower Tier)

Trinity Road Stand (Upper Tier)

STATISTICS

Final Standings 03-04
Pos		W	D	L	Pts
5	Newcastle	13	17	8	56
6	**Aston Villa**	**15**	**11**	**12**	**56**
7	Charlton	14	11	13	53

All-Time Record
League matches only (home and away)

Played	Won
136	**52**

Drawn	Lost
30	**54**

Last Five Meetings
10/04/2004 Premiership
Bolton Wanderers 2-2 Aston Villa
Scorers: Pedersen 48, Davies 86

27/01/2004 League Cup
Aston Villa 2-0 Bolton Wanderers

21/01/2004 League Cup
Bolton Wanderers 5-2 Aston Villa
Scorers: Okocha 2,80, Nolan 9, Stelios 17, N'Gotty 74

05/10/2003 Premiership
Aston Villa 1-1 Bolton Wanderers
Scorer: Nolan 46

01/01/2003 Premiership
Aston Villa 2-0 Bolton Wanderers

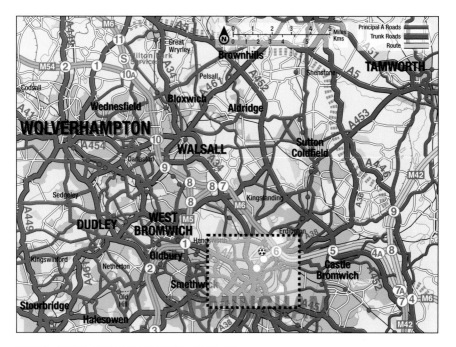

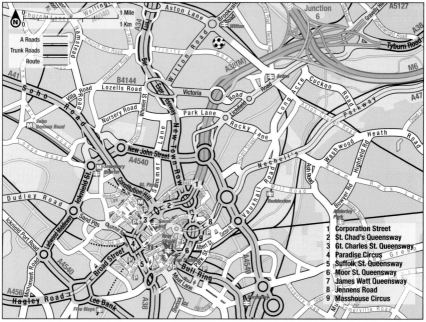

1 Corporation Street
2 St. Chad's Queensway
3 Gt. Charles St. Queensway
4 Paradise Circus
5 Suffolk St. Queensway
6 Moor St. Queensway
7 James Watt Queensway
8 Jennens Road
9 Masshouse Circus

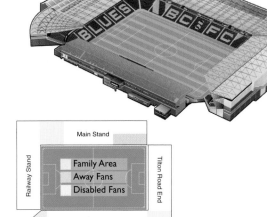

Birmingham City

Useful Information

Website: www.bcfc.com
Address: St Andrew's Stadium, Birmingham B9 4NH
Main Switchboard: 0121 772 0101

Travel Information

By Train: PBirmingham New Street and Birmingham Moor Street are both roughly 20 minutes walk from the ground. Taxis from the station to the ground cost around £3.50.
By Bus: Numbers 56, 57, 57a, 58 and 60 run from the city centre to the ground. Numbers 15, 17, 96 and 97 also stop near the stadium.

Main Stand

Railway Stand

Family Area
Away Fans
Disabled Fans

Tilton Road End

Kop Stand

STATISTICS

Final Standings 03-04

Pos		W	D	L	Pts
9	Fulham	14	10	14	52
10	**Birmingham**	**12**	**14**	**12**	**50**
11	Middlesbrough	13	9	16	48

All-Time Record

League matches only (home and away)

Played	Won
106	**41**

Drawn	Lost
30	**35**

Last Five Meetings

06/03/2004 Premiership
Birmingham City 2-0 Bolton Wanderers

25/10/2003 Premiership
Bolton Wanderers 0-1 Birmingham City

01/02/2003 Premiership
Bolton Wanderers 4-2 Birmingham City
Scorers: Cunningham 12 (og), Pedersen 46, Djorkaeff 84, Facey 87

02/11/2002 Premiership
Birmingham City 3-1 Bolton Wanderers
Scorer: Okocha 72

13/04/2001 Division One
Bolton Wanderers 2-2 Birmingham City
Scorers: Bergsson 53, Holdsworth 55

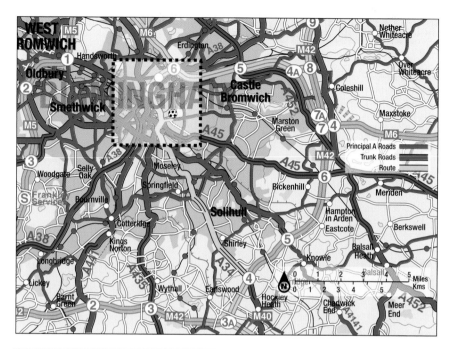

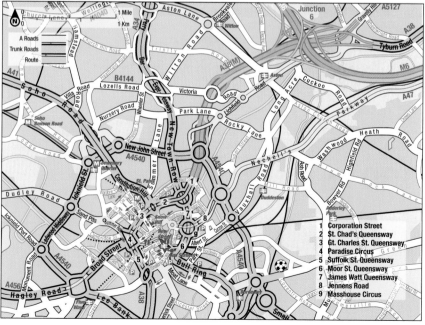

1 Corporation Street
2 St. Chad's Queensway
3 Gt. Charles St. Queensway
4 Paradise Circus
5 Suffolk St. Queensway
6 Moor St. Queensway
7 James Watt Queensway
8 Jennens Road
9 Masshouse Circus

Blackburn Rovers

Useful Information

Website: www.rovers.co.uk
Address: Ewood Park, Blackburn,
Lancashire BB2 4JF
Main Switchboard: 08701 113232

Travel Information

Car Parking: Car parking can be found
immediately adjacent to the stadium for up
to 800 vehicles; there are three other car
parks on Albion St, Albion Rd and Branch Rd
on the industrial estates. Street parking is
very limited.
By Train: Blackburn station is approx 1 1/2
miles away, Mill Hill is approx 1 mile away.
By Bus: There are 3 matchday services
that run from Accrington (Route A), Intack
(Route B) and Darwen (Route C). This service
costs £2.00 for a return ticket. Tickets are
not interchangeable between routes.

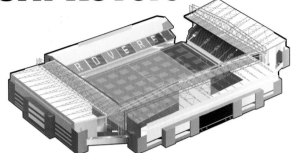

```
                    CIS Stand

Blackburn Stand    [ ] Family Area
(Lower Tier)       [ ] Away Fans        Darwen End / International Suite / Darwen End
                   [ ] Disabled Fans    (Lower Tier) (Upper Tier)        (Upper Tier)

       Jack Walker Stand (Lower Tier)
   Premier Suite  |  Centenary Suite
       Jack Walker Stand (Upper Tier)
```

STATISTICS

Final Standings 03-04

Pos		W	D	L	Pts
14	Tottenham	13	6	19	45
15	**Blackburn**	**12**	**8**	**18**	**44**
16	Man City	9	14	15	41

All-Time Record

League matches only (home and away)

Played	Won
130	**54**

Drawn	Lost
29	**47**

Last Five Meetings

10/01/2004 Premiership
Blackburn Rovers 3-4 Bolton Wanderers
Scorers: Nolan 1, 78, Djorkaeff 43, Stelios 73

23/08/2003 Premiership
Bolton Wanderers 2-2 Blackburn Rovers
Scorers: Djorkaeff 3 (pen), Davies 25

21/04/2003 Premiership
Blackburn Rovers 0-0 Bolton Wanderers

07/12/2002 Premiership
Bolton Wanderers 1-1 Blackburn Rovers
Scorer: Okocha 8

02/03/2002 Premiership
Bolton Wanderers 1-1 Blackburn Rovers
Scorer: Wallace 45

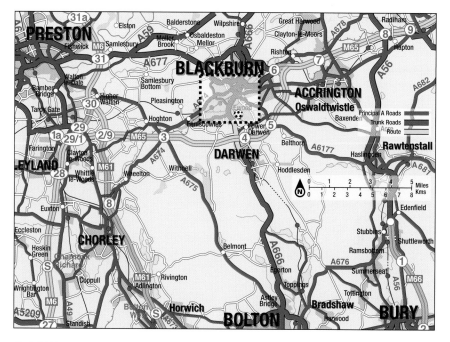

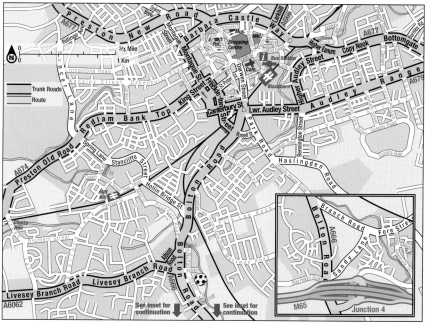

⬣ Charlton Athletic

Useful Information

Website: www.cafc.co.uk
Address: The Valley, Floyd Road, Charlton, London SE7 8BL
Main Switchboard: 020 8333 4000

Travel Information

Car Parking: Parking is available on Victoria Way, an 8 minute walk from the ground. It costs £5 and payment is on the gate. Street parking is very limited around the ground and public transport is recommended.

By Train: Trains run from Charing Cross, London Bridge and Waterloo East to Charlton station, approx. 2 minutes walk. Turn right out of station and the left into Floyd Road. North Greenwich on the Jubilee Line has bus links to the ground.

By Bus: Numbers 177 (towards Peckham), 180 (towards Lewisham), 53 (towards Plumstead) or 54 (toward Woolwich). 161, 422, 472, 486 (towards North Greenwich).

West Stand (Upper Tier)	NorthWest Quadrant
West Stand (Lower Tier)	

South Stand	Family Area	North Stand
	Away Fans	
	Disabled Fans	

East Stand	NorthEast Quadrant

STATISTICS

Final Standings 03-04

Pos		W	D	L	Pts
6	Aston Villa	15	11	12	56
7	**Charlton**	**14**	**11**	**13**	**53**
8	Bolton	14	11	13	53

All-Time Record

League matches only (home and away)

Played	Won
68	**33**

Drawn	Lost
12	**23**

Last Five Meetings

31/01/2004 Premiership
Charlton Athletic 1-2 Bolton Wanderers
Scorers: Pedersen 1, Nolan 78

30/08/2003 Premiership
Bolton Wanderers 0-0 Charlton Athletic

18/01/2003 Premiership
Charlton Athletic 1-1 Bolton Wanderers
Scorer: Djorkaeff 85

24/08/2002 Premiership
Bolton Wanderers 1-2 Charlton Athletic
Scorer: Djorkaeff 2

23/03/2002 Premiership
Charlton Athletic 1-2 Bolton Wanderers
Scorers: Djorkaeff 15, 39

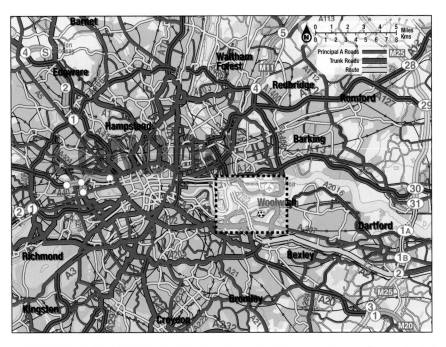

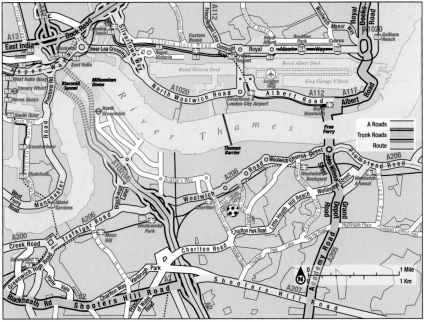

Chelsea

Useful Information
Website: www.chelseafc.com
Address: Stamford Bridge, Fulham Road, London SW6 1HS
Main Switchboard: 020 7385 5545

Travel Information
Car Parking: Parking restrictions during the game make it advisable to travel by tube. Limited on-site matchday underground parking is available in advance: 0207 915 1956
By Tube: Fulham Broadway is on the District Line, approx 5 minutes walk. Turn left out of station and ground is on the left hand side.
By Bus: Numbers 14 (towards Tottenham Court Road), 414 and 211 (towards Hammersmith) go along Fulham Road. Numbers 11, 14, 28, 211, 295, 391, 414, 424 all stop near the ground.

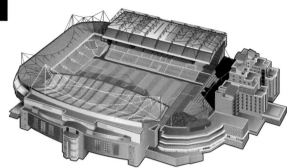

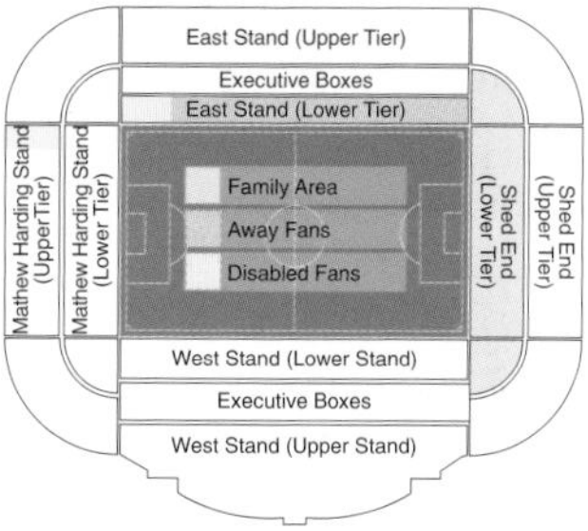

East Stand (Upper Tier)	
Executive Boxes	
East Stand (Lower Tier)	
Family Area	
Away Fans	
Disabled Fans	
West Stand (Lower Stand)	
Executive Boxes	
West Stand (Upper Stand)	

(Side labels: Mathew Harding Stand (Upper Tier), Mathew Harding Stand (Lower Tier); Shed End (Lower Tier), Shed End (Upper Tier), Shed End (Upper Tier))

STATISTICS

Final Standings 03-04
Pos		W	D	L	Pts
1	Arsenal	26	12	0	90
2	**Chelsea**	**24**	**7**	**7**	**79**
3	Man Utd	23	6	9	75

All-Time Record
League matches only (home and away)

Played	Won
92	**34**

Drawn	Lost
24	**34**

Last Five Meetings
13/03/2004 Premiership
Bolton Wanderers 0-2 Chelsea

13/12/2003 Premiership
Chelsea 1-2 Bolton Wanderers
Scorers: N'Gotty 39, Terry 90 (og)

12/04/2003 Premiership
Chelsea 1-0 Bolton Wanderers

23/11/2002 Premiership
Bolton Wanderers 1-1 Chelsea
Scorer: Pedersen 63

12/01/2002 Premiership
Bolton Wanderers 2-2 Chelsea
Scorers: Ricketts 56, Nolan 79

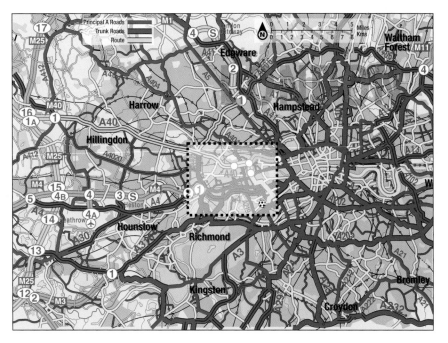

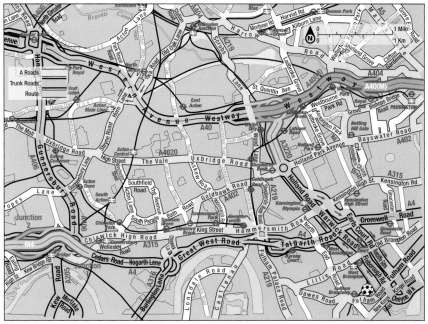

# Crystal Palace

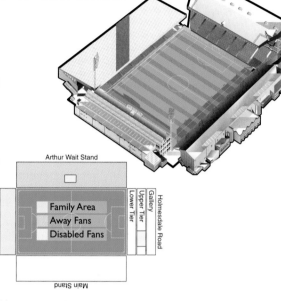

Useful Information

Website: www.cpfc.co.uk
Address: Selhurst Park, South Norwood, London SE25 6PU
Main Switchboard: 020 8768 6000

Travel Information

By Train:
Thornton Heath, Selhurst and Norwood Junction stations are all a five-minute walk from the ground. Trains run from Victoria or London Bridge.

By Bus:
Numbers 468, 196 and 410.

Arthur Wait Stand

Whitehorse Lane Stand
Executive Boxes

Family Area
Away Fans
Disabled Fans

Lower Tier
Upper Tier
Gallery
Holmesdale Road

Main Stand

STATISTICS

Final Standings 03-04

Pos		W	D	L	Pts
5	Ipswich	21	10	15	73
6	**C Palace**	**21**	**10**	**15**	**73**
7	Wigan	18	17	11	71

All-Time Record
League matches only (home and away)

Played	Won
32	**11**

Drawn	Lost
14	**7**

Last Five Meetings

16/04/2001 Division One
Crystal Palace 0-2 Bolton Wanderers
Scorers: Marshall 12, Summerbee 68

28/10/2000 Division One
Bolton Wanderers 3-3 Crystal Palace
Scorers: Bergsson 20, Ricketts 75, Frandsen 77

07/03/2000 Division One
Crystal Palace 0-0 Bolton Wanderers

06/11/1999 Division One
Bolton Wanderers 2-0 Crystal Palace
Scorers: Gudjohnsen 64, Jensen 82

10/01/1999 Division One
Bolton Wanderers 3-0 Crystal Palace
Scorers: Taylor 3, Gudjohnsen 26, Jensen 33

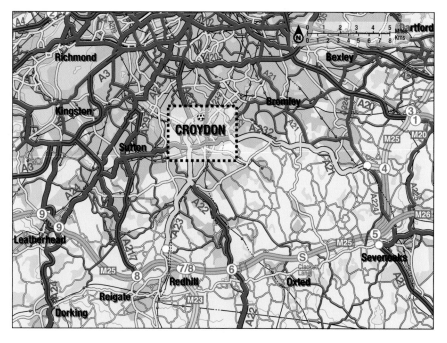

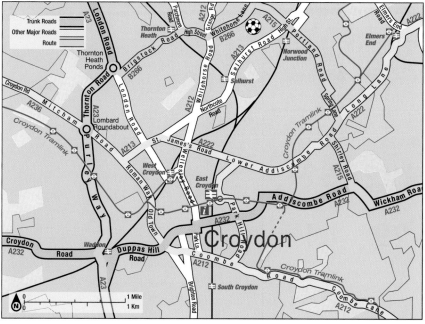

Everton

Useful Information
Website: evertonfc.com
Address: Goodison Park, Liverpool L4 4EL
Main Switchboard: 0151 330 2200

Travel Information
Car Parking: 1000 spaces are available at Stanley Park, costing £6. Street parking is residents only
By Train: Take any train from Liverpool Central which is heading for Ormskirk or Kirkby and alight at Kirkdale, a 10 minute walk from the ground.
By Bus: The number 19 runs from the Queen's Square bus station to Walton Lane; the number 20 runs along Spellow Lane.

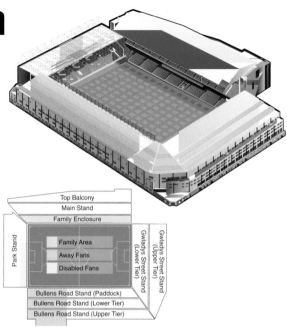

STATISTICS

Final Standings 03-04

Pos		W	D	L	Pts
16	Man City	9	14	15	41
17	**Everton**	**9**	**12**	**17**	**39**
18	Leicester	6	15	17	33

All-Time Record
League matches only (home and away)

Played	Won
122	**32**

Drawn	Lost
29	**61**

Last Five Meetings

08/05/2004 Premiership
Everton 1-2 Bolton Wanderers
Scorers: Djorkaeff 14, 87

29/11/2003 Premiership
Bolton Wanderers 2-0 Everton
Scorers: Frandsen 26, Djorkaeff 46

28/01/2003 Premiership
Bolton Wanderers 1-2 Everton
Scorer: Bergsson 90

28/12/2002 Premiership
Everton 0-0 Bolton Wanderers

01/04/2002 Premiership
Everton 3-1 Bolton Wanderers
Scorer: N'Gotty 75

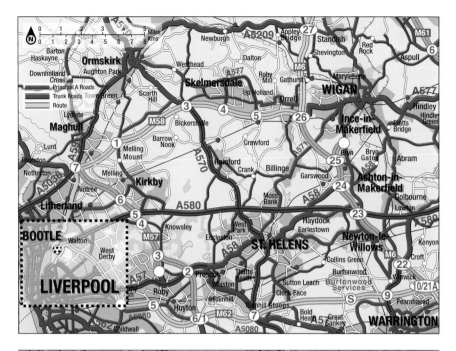

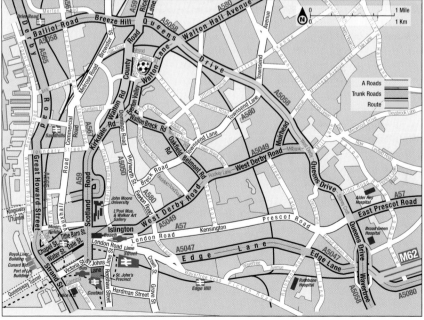

Fulham

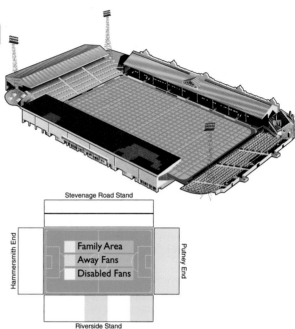

Stevenage Road Stand

Hammersmith End

Family Area
Away Fans
Disabled Fans

Putney End

Riverside Stand

Useful Information

Website: www.fulhamfc.com
Address: Craven Cottage, Stevenage Road, Fulham, London SW6 6HH
Main Switchboard: 0870 442 1222

Travel Information

Car Parking: There is very limited car parking on matchdays, so public transport is recommended for visiting supporters.

By Tube: Craven Cottage is a 10 minute walk from Putney Bridge station, which is on the Wimbledon branch of the District Line.

By Bus: Numbers 74 (to Roehampton) and 220 (to Wandsworth) both pass outside the ground.

STATISTICS

Final Standings 03-04

Pos		W	D	L	Pts
8	Bolton	14	11	13	53
9	**Fulham**	**14**	**10**	**14**	**52**
10	Birmingham	12	14	12	50

All-Time Record

League matches only (home and away)

Played	Won
60	**24**

Drawn	Lost
16	**20**

Last Five Meetings

15/05/2004 Premiership
Bolton Wanderers 0-2 Fulham

06/12/2003 Premiership
Fulham 2-1 Bolton Wanderers
Scorer: Davies 53

11/01/2003 Premiership
Bolton Wanderers 0-0 Fulham

17/08/2002 Premiership
Fulham 4-1 Bolton Wanderers
Scorer: Ricketts 4 (pen)

23/04/2002 Premiership
Fulham 3-0 Bolton Wanderers

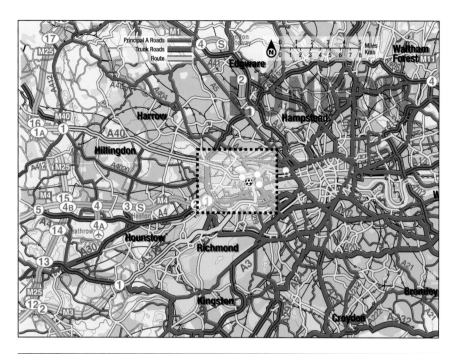

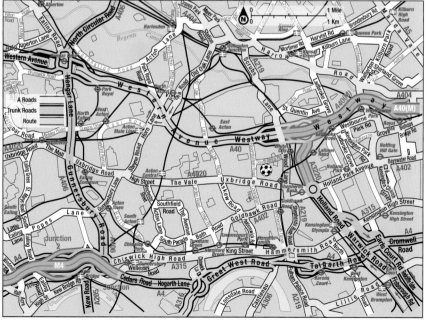

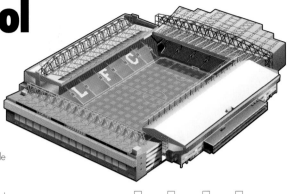

Liverpool

Useful Information
Website: www.liverpoolfc.tv
Address: Anfield Road, Liverpool L4 0TH
Main Switchboard: 0151 263 2361

Travel Information
By Train: Lime Street Railway Station
is in the town centre, 2 miles from Anfield. Kirkdale
Railway Station is 30 minutes walk from the
ground. Frequent Soccerbus shuttles run from
Sandhills Station two hours before each match and
50 minutes after the final whistle.

By Bus: Numbers 26 and 27 run from Paradise
Street bus station. Numbers 5, 17b, 17c, 17d
and 217 run from Queen Square bus station.
There is a 'Soccerbus' service that runs from
Sandhills station to Anfield for two hours before the
match and 50 minutes afterwards.

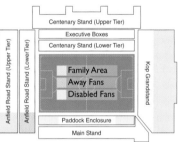

STATISTICS

Final Standings 03-04

Pos		W	D	L	Pts
3	Man Utd	23	6	9	75
4	**Liverpool**	**16**	**12**	**10**	**60**
5	Newcastle	13	17	8	56

All-Time Record
League matches only (home and away)

Played	Won
102	**33**

Drawn	Lost
28	**41**

Last Five Meetings

07/02/2004 Premiership
Bolton Wanderers 2-2 Liverpool
Scorers: Hunt 11, Djorkaeff 58

26/12/2003 Premiership
Liverpool 3-1 Bolton Wanderers
Scorer: Pedersen 85

03/12/2003 League Cup
Liverpool 2-3 Bolton Wanderers
Scorers: Jardel 4, Okocha 79, Djorkaeff 90 (pen)

08/03/2003 Premiership
Liverpool 2-0 Bolton Wanderers

14/09/2002 Premiership
Bolton Wanderers 2-3 Liverpool
Scorers: Gardner 54, Campo 87

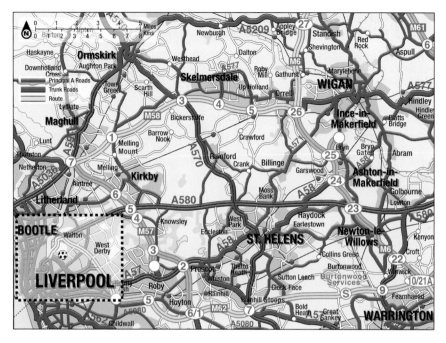

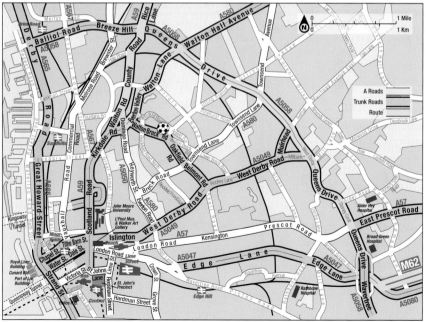

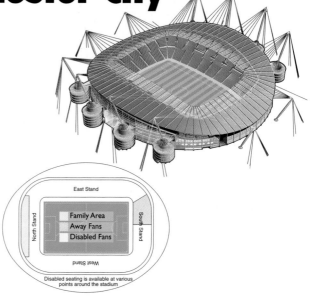

Manchester City

Useful Information

Website: www.mcfc.co.uk
Address: City of Manchester Stadium, Sportcity, Manchester M11 3FF
Main Switchboard: 0161 231 3200

Travel Information

By Train: The nearest station is Manchester Picadilly, approx 1 mile from the stadium
By Bus: Numbers 216, 217, and 230 to 237 run from the city centre

East Stand

North Stand

Family Area
Away Fans
Disabled Fans

South Stand

West Stand

Disabled seating is available at various points around the stadium

STATISTICS

Final Standings 03-04

Pos		W	D	L	Pts
15	Blackburn	12	8	18	44
16	**Man City**	**9**	**14**	**15**	**41**
17	Everton	9	12	17	39

All-Time Record

League matches only (home and away)

Played	Won
96	**36**

Drawn	Lost
22	**38**

Last Five Meetings

21/02/2004 Premiership
Bolton Wanderers 1-3 Manchester City
Scorer: Nolan 22

18/10/2003 Premiership
Manchester City 6-2 Bolton Wanderers
Scorers: Nolan 25, Campo 60

05/04/2003 Premiership
Bolton Wanderers 2-0 Manchester City
Scorers: Pedersen 32, Campo 52

30/11/2002 Premiership
Manchester City 2-0 Bolton Wanderers

05/04/2000 Division One
Manchester City 2-0 Bolton Wanderers

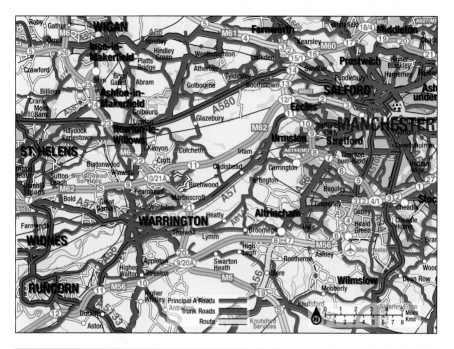

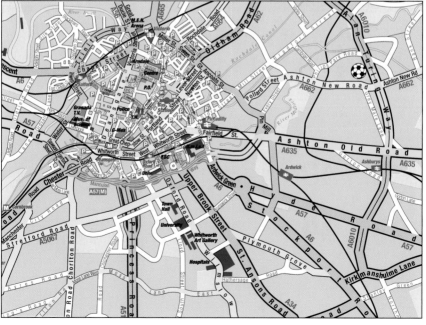

Manchester United

Useful Information
Website: manutd.com
Address: Sir Matt Busby Way, Old Trafford, Manchester M16 0RA
Main Switchboard: 0161 868 8000

Travel Information
Car Parking: There is a large official car park on Elevator Road, and various smaller car parks nearby.
By Metrolink: Old Trafford station is about 1/2 mile away from the ground.
By Train: (matchdays only): Special services run from the clubs own railway station adjacent to the south stand.
By Bus: Numbers 114, 230, 252 and 253 all run from the city centre to the ground.

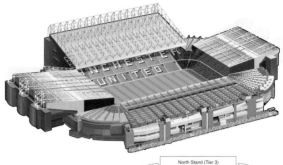

STATISTICS

Final Standings 03-04

Pos		W	D	L	Pts
2	Chelsea	24	7	7	79
3	**Man Utd**	23	6	9	75
4	Liverpool	16	12	10	60

All-Time Record
League matches only (home and away)

Played	Won
102	**40**

Drawn	Lost
23	**39**

Last Five Meetings

07/01/2004 Premiership
Bolton Wanderers 1-2 Manchester United
Scorer: Djorkaeff 89

16/08/2003 Premiership
Manchester United 4-0 Bolton Wanderers

22/02/2003 Premiership
Bolton Wanderers 1-1 Manchester United
Scorer: N'Gotty 61

11/09/2002 Premiership
Manchester United 0-1 Bolton Wanderers
Scorer: Nolan 76

29/01/2002 Premiership
Bolton Wanderers 0-4 Manchester United

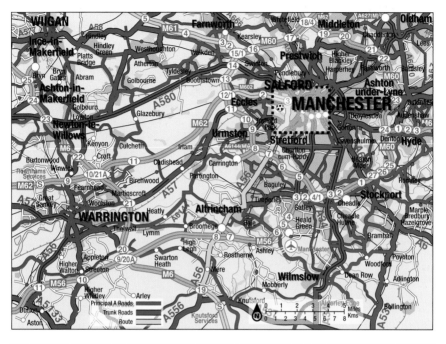

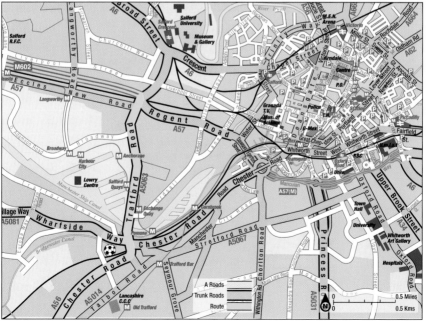

Middlesbrough

Useful Information
Website: www.mfc.co.uk
Address: Riverside Stadium,
Middlesbrough, Cleveland TS3 6RS
Main Switchboard: 01642 877700

Travel Information
Car Parking: There are various multi-storey car parks in the town centre, which fans are encouraged to use and walk to the ground, approx 15 minutes away.

By Train: Middlesbrough station is about 15 minutes walk from the ground, take the back exit from the station, turn right, then after a couple of minutes right again into Windward Way.

By Bus: The numbers 36, 37 and 38 go from the town centre to within a short walking distance of the ground.

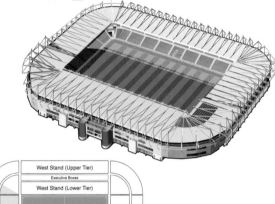

| West Stand (Upper Tier) |
| Executive Boxes |
| West Stand (Lower Tier) |
| Family Area |
| Away Fans |
| Disabled Fans |
| East Stand (Lower Tier) |
| East Stand (Upper Tier) |

South Stand (Upper Tier) · South Stand (Lower Tier) · North Stand (Lower Tier) · North Stand (Upper Tier)

STATISTICS

Final Standings 03-04

Pos		W	D	L	Pts
10	Birmingham	12	14	12	50
11	**Middlesbrough**	**13**	**9**	**16**	**48**
12	Southampton	12	11	15	47

All-Time Record
League matches only (home and away)

Played	Won
98	**46**

Drawn	Lost
22	**30**

Last Five Meetings

03/04/2004 Premiership
Middlesbrough 2-0 Bolton Wanderers

29/02/2004 League Cup
Bolton Wanderers 1-2 Middlesbrough
Scorer: Davies 21

13/09/2003 Premiership
Bolton Wanderers 2-0 Middlesbrough
Scorers: Davies 23, N'Gotty 81

11/05/2003 Premiership
Bolton Wanderers 2-1 Middlesbrough
Scorers: Frandsen 10, Okocha 21

05/10/2002 Premiership
Middlesbrough 2-0 Bolton Wanderers

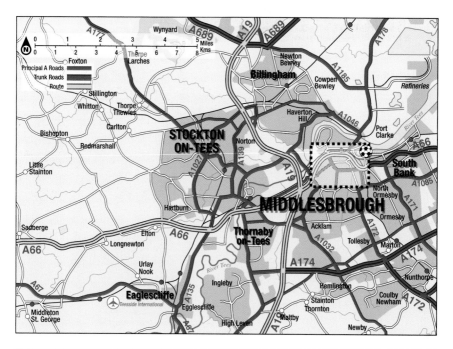

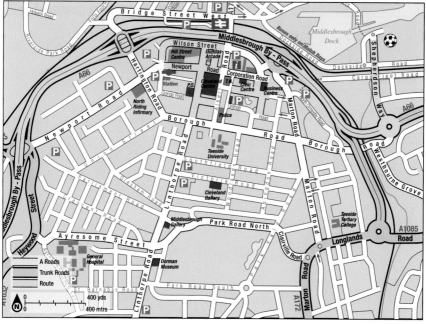

Newcastle United

Useful Information

Website: www.nufc.co.uk

Address: St James' Park,
Newcastle-upon-Tyne NE1 4ST

Main Switchboard: 0191 201 8400

Travel Information

Car Parking: There is no parking within
the confines of St. James' Park. However there are
extensive parking facilities in the City Centre which
is a very short walk to the stadium.

By Train: St James' Park is a short 5-minute walk
from the British Rail Central Station. Turn left out
of the station onto Neville Street, past two sets of
lights and right into St James' Boulevard. You will
be able to see St. James' Park ahead of you at
the top of St. James' Boulevard. The stadium is
also served by its own Metro station adjacent to
the ground (St James Metro).

By Bus: Catch a bus from the town centre
heading towards Gallowgate.

STATISTICS

Final Standings 03-04

Pos		W	D	L	Pts
4	Liverpool	16	12	10	60
5	**Newcastle**	**13**	**17**	**8**	**56**
6	Aston Villa	15	11	12	56

All-Time Record

League matches only (home and away)

Played	Won
108	**35**

Drawn	Lost
17	**56**

Last Five Meetings

28/03/2004 Premiership
Bolton Wanderers 1-0 Newcastle United
Scorer: Pedersen 4

20/09/2003 Premiership
Newcastle United 0-0 Bolton Wanderers

22/01/2003 Premiership
Newcastle United 1-0 Bolton Wanderers

26/12/2002 Premiership
Bolton Wanderers 4-3 Newcastle United
Scorers: Okocha 5, Gardner 9, Ricketts 45, 63

02/02/2002 Premiership
Newcastle United 3-2 Bolton Wanderers
Scorers: Gardner 19, Southall 34

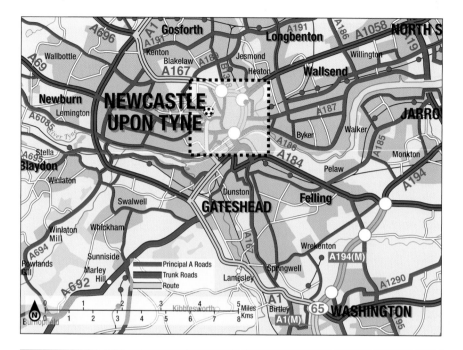

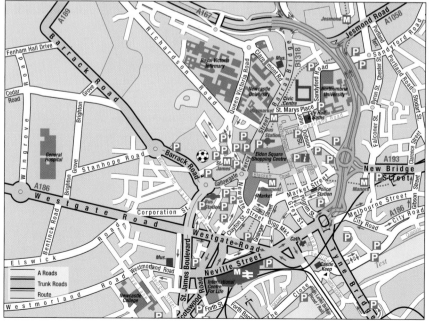

Norwich City

Useful Information
Website: www.canaries.co.uk
Address: Carrow Road,
Norwich NR1 1JE
Main Switchboard: 01603 760 760

Travel Information
Car Parking:
There are designated car parks in the
surrounding area.
By Train:
Norwich station in within walking distance
(approx 10 minutes) of Carrow Road.

South Stand

Barclay Stand
Upper
Lower

Family Area
Away Fans
Disabled Fans

Lower
Upper
Executive Boxes

Goffrey Watling City Stand

STATISTICS

Final Standings 03-04

Pos		W	D	L	Pts
1	Norwich	28	10	8	94
2	West Brom	25	11	10	86
3	Sunderland	22	13	11	79

All-Time Record
League matches only (home and away)

Played	Won
32	**12**

Drawn	Lost
8	**12**

Last Five Meetings

21/04/2001 Division One
Bolton Wanderers 1-0 Norwich City
Scorer: Holdsworth 66

18/11/2000 Division One
Norwich City 0-2 Bolton Wanderers
Scorers: Ricketts 58, Bergsson 74

07/05/2000 Division One
Bolton Wanderers 1-0 Norwich City
Scorer: Holdsworth 72

24/10/1999 Division One
Norwich City 2-1 Bolton Wanderers
Scorer: Gardner 74

20/04/1999 Division One
Norwich City 2-2 Bolton Wanderers
Scorers: Cox 48, Frandsen 74

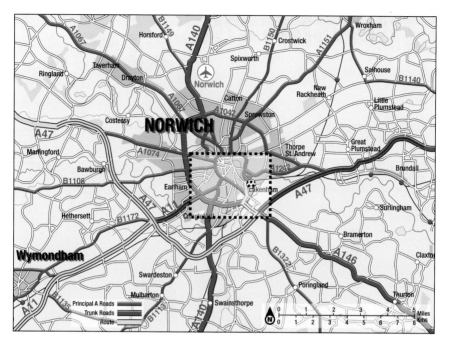

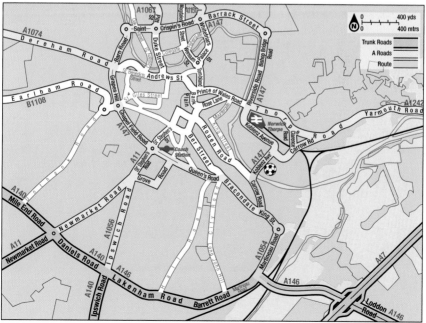

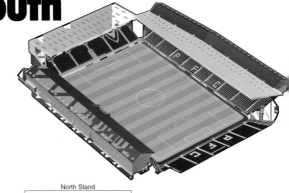

Portsmouth

Useful Information
Website: www.pompeyfc.co.uk
Address: Fratton Park, Frogmore Road,
Portsmouth PO4 8RA
Main Switchboard:
023 9273 1204

Travel Information
By Train: Fratton station is a short walk
from the ground
By Bus: Numbers 3, 13, 14, 16a,
24, 27 and 57 all run to Fratton station.

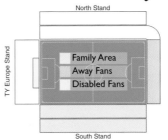

North Stand

TY Europe Stand

| Family Area |
| Away Fans |
| Disabled Fans |

South Stand

STATISTICS

Final Standings 03-04
Pos		W	D	L	Pts
12	Southampton	12	11	15	47
13	**Portsmouth**	**12**	**9**	**17**	**45**
14	Tottenham	13	6	19	45

All-Time Record
League matches only (home and away)

Played	Won
80	**35**

Drawn	Lost
18	**27**

Last Five Meetings
17/01/2004 Premiership
Bolton Wanderers 1-0 Portsmouth
Scorer: Davies 53

26/08/2003 Premiership
Portsmouth 4-0 Bolton Wanderers

13/02/2001 Division One
Portsmouth 1-2 Bolton Wanderers
Scorers: Ricketts 48, Hansen 71

16/09/2000 Division One
Bolton Wanderers 2-0 Portsmouth
Scorers: Holdsworth 42, Ricketts 85

22/02/2000 Division One
Bolton Wanderers 3-0 Portsmouth
Scorers: Taylor 12, Jensen 68, Elliott 77

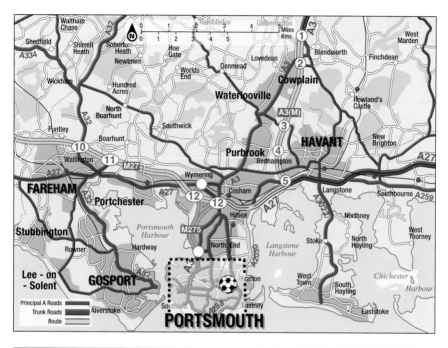

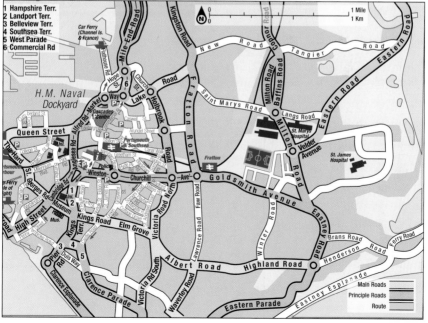

1 Hampshire Terr.
2 Landport Terr.
3 Belleview Terr.
4 Southsea Terr.
5 West Parade
6 Commercial Rd

Southampton

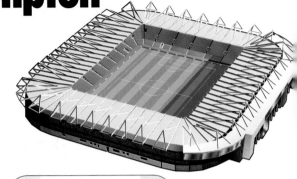

Useful Information
Website: www.saintsfc.co.uk
Address: The Friends Provident St Mary's Stadium, Britannia Road, Southampton, Hants SO14 5FP
Main Switchboard: 0870 220 0000

Travel Information
Car Parking: The club urge people not to head towards the stadium by car as the surrounding area is subject to police restrictions. Parking for both home and visiting supporters maybe available, but bookings must be made in advance. Please phone 0870 220 0150 for details.
By Train/Bus: The nearest station to the ground is Southampton Central. Shuttle buses run from the station to the stadium two hours before the game up until kick off.

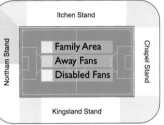

STATISTICS

Final Standings 03-04

Pos		W	D	L	Pts
11	Middlesbrough	13	9	16	48
12	**Southampton**	**12**	**11**	**15**	**47**
13	Portsmouth	12	9	17	45

All-Time Record
League matches only (home and away)

Played	Won
30	**13**

Drawn	Lost
9	**8**

Last Five Meetings

24/04/2004 Premiership
Southampton 1-2 Bolton Wanderers
Scorers: Nolan 77, Davies 78

16/12/2003 League Cup
Bolton Wanderers 1-0 Southampton (AET)
Scorer: Pedersen 115

08/11/20-03 Premiership
Bolton Wanderers 0-0 Southampton

03/05/2003 Premiership
Southampton 0-0 Bolton Wanderers

28/09/2002 Premiership
Bolton Wanderers 1-1 Southampton
Scorer: Djorkaeff 90

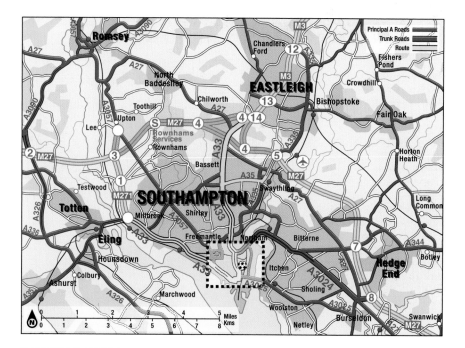

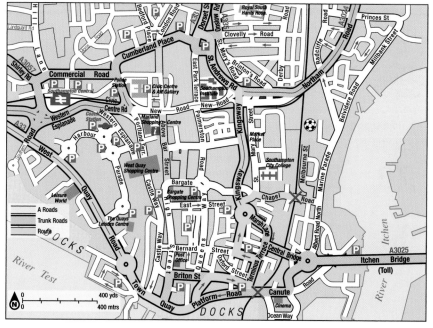

Tottenham Hotspur

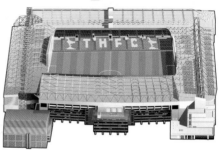

Useful Information
Website: www.spurs.co.uk
Address: Bill Nicholson Way, 748 High Road, Tottenham,
London N17 0AP
Main Switchboard: 020 8365 5000

Travel Information
Car Parking: Limited parking is available near the ground.
By Train/Tube: The nearest Underground station is Seven Sisters (Victoria Line), approx 30 minute walk.
The nearest station is White Hart Lane, approx 5 minutes walk, on the Liverpool Street-Enfield Town line.
By Bus: Numbers 149, 259 and 279 all go along Tottenham High Road.

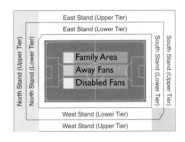

STATISTICS

Final Standings 03-04
Pos		W	D	L	Pts
13	Portsmouth	12	9	17	45
14	**Tottenham**	**13**	**6**	**19**	**45**
15	Blackburn	12	8	18	44

All-Time Record
League matches only (home and away)

Played	Won
72	**28**

Drawn	Lost
11	**33**

Last Five Meetings
17/04/2004 Premiership
Bolton Wanderers 2-0 Tottenham Hotspur
Scorers: Campo 7, Pedersen 65

01/11/2003 Premiership
Tottenham Hotspur 0-1 Bolton Wanderers
Scorer: Nolan 73

24/03/2003 Premiership
Bolton Wanderers 1-0 Tottenham Hotspur
Scorer: Okocha 90 (pen)

20/10/2002 Premiership
Tottenham Hotspur 3-1 Bolton Wanderers
Scorer: Djorkaeff 63

20/04/2002 Premiership
Bolton Wanderers 1-1 Tottenham Hotspur
Scorer: Holdsworth 71

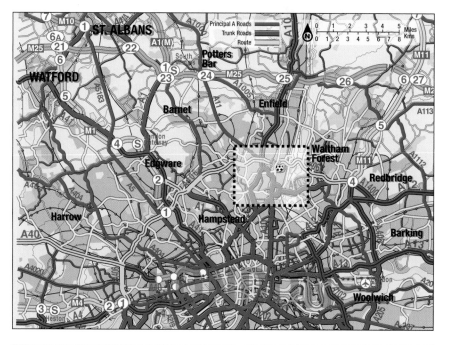

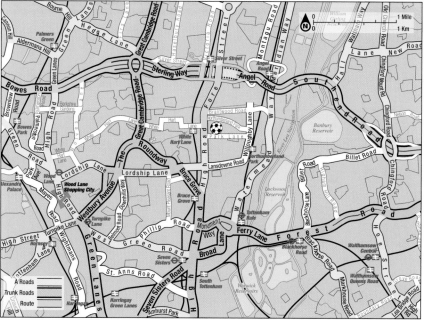

West Bromwich Albion

Useful Information
Website: www.wba.co.uk
Address: The Hawthorns, Halfords Lane,
West Bromwich, West Midlands B71 4LF
Main Switchboard: 0121 525 8888

Travel Information
Car Parking:
There is limited parking available
in the East Stand car park and the
surrounding streets.
By Train:
Trains run to Hawthorns station from Snow
Hill, which is a five minute walk from New
Street station, Birmingham.

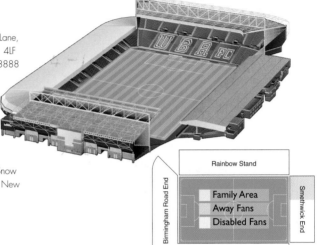

Rainbow Stand

Birmingham Road End

Family Area
Away Fans
Disabled Fans

Smethwick End

Halford's Lane (Main) Stand

STATISTICS

Final Standings 03-04

Pos		W	D	L	Pts
1	Norwich	28	10	8	94
2	**West Brom**	**25**	**11**	**10**	**86**
3	Sunderland	22	13	11	79

All-Time Record
League matches only (home and away)

Played	Won
124	**45**

Drawn	Lost
38	**41**

Last Five Meetings

08/02/2003 Premiership
West Bromwich Albion 1-1 Bolton Wanderers
Scorer: Pedersen 18

09/11/2003 Premiership
Bolton Wanderers 1-1 West Bromwich Albion
Scorer: Frandsen 89

17/05/2001 Division One Play-Off
Bolton Wanderers 3-0 West Bromwich Albion
Scorers: Bergsson 10, Gardner 63, Ricketts 90

13/05/2001 Division One Play-Off
West Bromwich Albion 2-2 Bolton Wanderers
Scorers: Bergsson 81, Frandsen 88 (pen)

30/12/2000 Division One
Bolton Wanderers 0-1 West Bromwich Albion

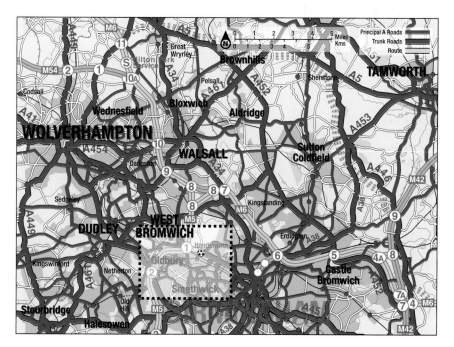

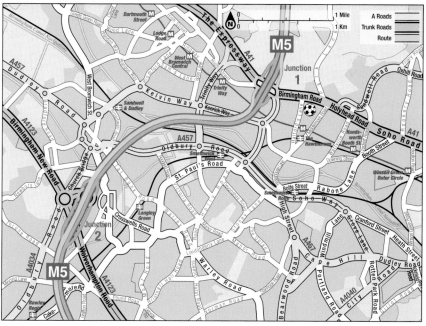

Enhanced Fixture List 2004-05

In this fixture...

Date	Opposition	03-04 score	Played	Premiership history	Goals for	Goals against	No. of times	⚽ ▶	Bolton scored first and the result that followed			Most common score (no. times)	Avg time of first goal (mins)	Avg no. of corners
									W	D	L			
14th Aug	Charlton	0 - 0	3	---------DLD *4 — 1 w*	1	2	1	▶	0	0	1	0-0 (2x)	2	8	*3*
21st Aug	Fulham	1 - 2	3	---------LLL *2 - 0 L*	2	9	2	▶	0	0	2	4-1 (1x)	29	2
25th Aug	Southampton	2 - 1	5	---L-W---DDW *1 - 2 w*	3	2	1	▶	1	0	0	0-0 (2x)	60	4	*6*
29th Aug	Liverpool	2 - 2	5	---L-D---WLD *1 - 0 w*	7	8	2	▶	1	1	0	2-3 (1x)	44	5	*9*
11th Sep	Man Utd	1 - 2	5	---L-D---LDL	2	13	1	▶	0	1	0	1-2 (1x)	75	8
18th Sep	Arsenal	1 - 2	5	---L-L---DLL	5	11	2	▶	0	0	2	2-1 (3x)	52	1
25th Sep	Birmingham	0 - 1	2	---------WL	4	3	1	▶	1	0	0	4-2 (1x)	12	5
2nd Oct	West Brom	n/a	1	----------D-	1	1	1	▶	0	1	0	1-1 (1x)	18	4
16th Oct	C Palace	n/a	1	-----W------	5	2	1	▶	1	0	0	5-2 (1x)	7	6
23rd Oct	Tottenham	1 - 0	5	---D-L---LLW	6	9	2	▶	1	0	1	3-2 (1x)	55	4
31st Oct	Newcastle	1 - 0	5	---L-W---LWW	7	10	3	▶	3	0	0	1-0 (2x)	21	7
7th Nov	Middlesbro	0 - 2	4	---W-----DLL	5	6	1	▶	1	0	0	2-0 (2x)	43	6
13th Nov	Aston Villa	2 - 2	5	---L-L---WWD	6	7	2	▶	2	0	0	3-2 (1x)	37	4
20th Nov	Chelsea	2 - 1	5	---L-L---LLW	5	12	2	▶	0	0	2	5-1 (1x)	17	5
27th Nov	Portsmouth	1 - 0	1	----------W	1	0	1	▶	1	0	0	1-0 (1x)	53	2
4th Dec	Everton	2 - 1	5	---L-L---LDW	5	10	1	▶	1	0	0	3-2 (1x)	44	3
11th Dec	Norwich	n/a		These teams have never played each other in the Premiership										
18th Dec	Man City	1 - 3	3	---D------WL	4	4	2	▶	1	0	1	2-0 (1x)	43	7
26th Dec	Man Utd	0 - 4	5	---L-D---WWL	4	9	2	▶	1	1	0	4-0 (1x)	57	4

Date	Opposition	03-04 score	Played	Premiership history	Goals for	Goals against	No. of times Bolton scored first and the result that followed					Most common score (no. times)	Avg time of first goal (mins)	Avg no. of corners	
							⚽	►	W	D	L				
28th Dec	Blackburn	2 - 2	5	---W-W---DDD	8	6	5	►	2	3	0	2-1 (2x)	19	5	🎽
1st Jan	West Brom	n/a	1	----------D-	1	1	0	►	0	0	0	1-1 (1x)	89	7	🎽
3rd Jan	Birmingham	0 - 2	2	----------LL	1	5	0	►	0	0	0	3-1 (1x)	72	5	
15th Jan	Arsenal	1 - 1	5	---W-L---LDD	4	6	1	►	1	0	0	2-2 (1x)	64	5	🎽
22nd Jan	Blackburn	4 - 3	5	---L-L---DDW	7	10	2	►	1	1	0	3-1 (2x)	46	4	
1st Feb	Tottenham	2 - 0	5	---L-D---DWW	7	5	3	►	2	1	0	1-1 (2x)	52	9	🎽
5th Feb	C Palace	n/a	1	-----D------	2	2	0	►	0	0	0	2-2 (1x)	36	5	
12th Feb	Middlesbro	2 - 0	4	---D-----WWW	6	2	4	►	3	1	0	2-1 (1x)	24	7	🎽
26th Feb	Newcastle	0 - 0	5	---L-L---LLD	4	8	1	►	0	0	1	2-1 (2x)	37	3	
5th Mar	Man City	2 - 6	3	---L------LL	2	9	1	►	0	0	1	6-2 (1x)	24	3	
19th Mar	Norwich	n/a	These teams have never played each other in the Premiership												🎽
2nd Apr	Liverpool	1 - 3	5	---L-L---DLL	5	13	1	►	0	0	1	5-2 (1x)	62	5	
9th Apr	Fulham	0 - 2	3	--------DDL	0	2	0	►	0	0	0	0-0 (2x)	N/A	6	🎽
16th Apr	Charlton	2 - 1	3	---------WDW	5	3	2	►	2	0	0	1-2 (2x)	34	4	
19th Apr	Southampton	0 - 0	5	---L-D---LDD	1	3	0	►	0	0	0	0-1 (2x)	90	8	🎽
23rd Apr	Aston Villa	1 - 1	5	---L-W---LLD	6	8	3	►	1	1	1	3-2 (1x)	22	4	
30th Apr	Chelsea	0 - 2	5	---W-W---DDL	6	6	2	►	1	1	0	2-2 (1x)	58	6	🎽
7th May	Portsmouth	0 - 4	1	----------L	0	4	0	►	0	0	0	4-0 (1x)	N/A	4	
14th May	Everton	2 - 0	5	---D-D---DLW	6	5	3	►	1	2	0	2-2 (1x)	32	6	🎽

Premiership Fixture Grid 2004-05

Home \ Away	West Brom	Tottenham H	Southampton	Portsmouth	Norwich City	Newcastle Utd	Middlesbrough	Manchester Utd	Manchester City	Liverpool	Fulham	Everton	Crystal Palace	Chelsea	Charlton	Bolton	Blackburn	Birmingham	Aston Villa	Arsenal
Arsenal	30/04	13/11	26/02	19/12	28/08	29/12	09/04	24/10	25/09	28/11	11/09	15/08	06/11	20/04	01/01	15/01	19/03	14/05	05/02	
Aston Villa	22/08	30/04	16/04	12/02	02/04	02/02	18/12	22/01	27/11	14/05	02/02	30/10	03/01	26/12	24/08	13/11	02/10	19/03		16/10
Birmingham	05/03	28/08	24/10	14/08	07/05	01/01	11/09	05/02	20/04	06/11	28/12	23/04	26/02	09/04	15/01	25/09	21/11		19/03	04/12
Blackburn	16/04	14/05	21/08	15/01	06/11	11/09	05/02	02/04	13/11	26/02	27/11	05/03	11/12	23/10	27/09	28/12		30/04	01/01	24/08
Bolton	02/10	23/10	25/08	07/05	11/12	26/02	07/11	26/12	05/03	02/04	21/08	04/12	05/02	20/11	05/12		22/01	03/01	18/09	02/10
Charlton	11/12	06/11	26/12	09/04	23/04	05/02	26/02	20/11	28/08	23/10	05/03	22/01	05/12	27/11		14/08	03/01	27/09	05/03	02/10
Chelsea	30/10	15/01	02/04	28/12	05/03	14/05	25/09	16/10	01/01	13/11	12/02	24/08	19/03		27/11	07/05	20/11	27/11	21/08	12/02
Crystal Palace	01/02	28/12	27/11	11/09	14/08	23/10	28/08	15/01	11/12	26/12	30/08	15/01		19/03	14/05	05/02	04/12	22/01	03/01	09/04
Everton	02/04	15/01	26/09	05/02	23/10	28/11	15/01	14/05	18/12	11/12	18/09		21/08	06/11	28/12	14/05	26/02	18/12	16/04	07/05
Fulham	18/09	26/02	03/01	30/08	04/12	06/11	19/04	19/03	14/08	05/02		20/11	04/10	23/04	20/12	09/04	07/05	07/05	23/10	26/12
Liverpool	26/12	02/02	14/08	04/12	06/11	20/12	20/11	20/09	09/04		16/10	11/12	23/04	01/01	03/01	05/03	05/03	02/04	30/10	26/12
Manchester City	22/01	19/03	02/10	20/11	26/02	23/10	06/12	14/11		21/08	16/04	26/12	18/09	05/02	02/04	07/05	24/08	07/05	03/01	22/01
Manchester Utd	27/11	25/09	14/05	30/10	09/04	14/11	01/01		12/02	15/01	13/12	20/04	05/03	15/08	30/04	11/09	28/08	16/10	28/12	01/02
Middlesbrough	14/11	27/11	11/12	01/02	22/01	16/04		02/10	14/05	30/04	19/03	02/04	03/01	30/10	18/09	16/10	12/02	26/12	05/03	22/08
Newcastle Utd	03/01	09/04	19/09	19/03	19/04		14/08	23/04	21/08	26/02	20/11	04/12	17/10	13/11	19/03	31/10	12/02	02/02	02/10	07/05
Norwich City	16/10	12/09	30/04	01/01		25/08	28/12	21/08	01/11	14/05	25/09	02/02	14/04	18/12	13/11	19/03	12/02	27/11	04/02	02/04
Portsmouth	05/03	23/10	26/02		02/10	11/12	23/10	26/02	03/01	26/12	22/01	21/08	28/12	02/04	25/09	18/09	14/08	26/12	09/04	05/03
Southampton	14/05	18/12		23/04	20/11	01/01	01/02	01/01	18/12	14/08	03/01	19/03	19/09	04/12	03/01	15/09	15/01	28/08	30/04	30/10
Tottenham H	12/02		18/12	12/09	09/04	27/11	11/12	25/09	19/03	14/08	26/02	05/03	12/12	19/04	09/04	26/12	12/02	01/02	06/11	13/11
West Brom		20/04	12/02	14/05	04/12	06/11	14/11	27/11	01/02	09/04	20/11	20/11	09/04	23/04	01/01	23/10	18/12	09/04	20/11	30/04